I0568495

The Only Law of Attraction Book You'll Ever Need

The Complete Guide to Manifesting Money, Love, Health, and Anything You Want in Life

Layla Moon

The Only Law of Attraction Book You'll Ever Need

The Only Law of Attraction Book You'll Ever Need

Table of Contents

4 FREE Gifts

To help you along your spiritual journey, I've created 4 FREE bonu4 FREE Giftss eBooks.

You can get instant access by signing up to my email newsletter below.

On top of the 4 free books, you will also receive weekly tips along with free book giveaways, discounts, and so much more.

All of these bonuses are 100% free with no strings attached. You don't need to provide any personal information except your email address.

To get your bonus, go to:

https://dreamlifepress.com/four-free-gifts

Or scan the QR code below

SCAN ME

Spirit Guides for Beginners: How to Hear the Universe's Call and Communicate with Your Spirit Guide and Guardian Angels

Guided by Moon herself, inspired by her own experiences and knowledge that has been passed down by hundreds of generations for thousands of years, you'll discover everything you need to know to;

- Understanding what the call of the universe is
- How to hear and comprehend it
- Knowing who and what your spirit guides and guardian angels are
- Learning how to connect, start a conversation, and listen to your guides
- How to manifest your dreams with the help of the cosmic source
- Learning how to start living the life you want to live
- And so much more…

Law of Attraction: Manifest Your Desire

Learn how to tap into the infinite power of the universe and manifest everything you want in life.

Includes:

- Law of Attraction: Manifest Your Desire ebook
- Law of Attraction Workbook
- Cheat sheets and checklists so make sure you're on the right path

Hoodoo Book of Spells for Beginners: Easy and effective Rootwork, Conjuring, and Protection Spells for Healing and Prosperity

Harness the power of one of the greatest magics. Hoodoo is a powerful force ideal for holding negativity at bay, promoting positivity in all areas in your life, offering protection to the things you love, and ultimately taking control of your destiny.

Inside, you will discover:
- How to get started with Hoodoo in your day-to-day life
- How to use conjuration spells to manifest the life you want to live
- How casting protection spells can help you withstand the toughest of times
- Break cycles of bad luck and promote good fortune throughout your life
- Hoodoo to encourage prosperity and financial stability
- How to heal using Hoodoo magic, both short-term and long-term traumas and troubles
- Remove curses and banish pain, suffering, and negativity from your life
- And so much more...

4

Book of Shadows

A printable PDF to support you in your spiritual transformation.

Within the pages, you will find:

- Potion and tinctures tracking sheet
- Essential oils log pages
- Herbs log pages
- Magical rituals and spiritual body goals checklist
- Tarot reading spread sheets
- Weekly moon and planetary cycle tracker
- And so much more

Get all the resources for FREE by visiting the link below

https://dreamlifepress.com/four-free-gifts

CHAPTER ONE

Introduction

What you think you become. What you feel you attract. What you imagine you create.
- Buddha

Finally. The last book you'll ever need when it comes to the law of attraction. It's right here in your hands. For the last two decades, I've made my way through this world, starting from rock bottom and working my way up to a place where I can actually be proud of myself. A place that I am happy to be. However, this book is not about my journey.

It's about yours.

What you hold in your hands is your complete guide to the Law of Attraction. A guide designed to help you live your best life. Have you ever wondered how to do that? Have you ever found yourself in a never-ending rut that you can never seem to pull yourself out of? Does it feel like life is holding you down by throwing one thing after another your way? Ever wondered about the best way to approach things when the going gets tough? Have you ever wanted to know how to put yourself on a path you can be proud of; to live a life you're content with?

The answers to all these questions lie within the Law of Attraction. Some call it a methodology. Some call it the secret. However you want to refer to it, there's no doubt that as you make your way through these pages, you're going to learn everything you need to know about taking control of your life, perhaps for the first time.

Now, to be clear, this is the last book you'll ever need to read when it comes to the Law of Attraction. You've probably read articles online or Rhonda Bryne's bestseller, and while they're great books, I found them impossibly more complex and spiritual than they needed to be. I loved them, but something was missing, at least for me and many other people I've spoken to about the subject.

If you're new to the Law of Attraction, this is a guidebook full of actionable takeaways that will change your life. These pages contain years of personal research, experience, trial and error, and ups and downs.

It's the definition of the Law of Attraction, what it stands for, how it works, and how you can use it to create and manifest the life you want.

This book is designed to help you stop wasting your time reading other books, attending random seminars, chatting with therapists and life coaches, instead enabling you to invest your time in taking action. Everything I've learned over the last two decades in one place. I have never found a source of teaching that fully encapsulates how you can make the Law of Attraction work for you practically.

So I set about writing my own. Here it is.

Where It All Began

To set the stage, here's my experience with the Law of Attraction This is a short section to start things off, so you know who I am and where I came from. More importantly, you can experience how the Law of Attraction quite literally changed my life.

Let's start at the beginning. About 15 years ago, I was in a rut. A low ebb, if you would. I was in my early twenties, living with an emotionally abusive partner, and our relationship was constantly teetering on the edge of breaking up. I was isolated from the world. I had few friends (or at least I didn't see them often), I was in a dead-end job, and to put it frankly, I hated myself. I'd go as far as saying 'despised.'

I remember looking in the mirror one day before leaving my dirty apartment and shaking my head at myself in the mirror. Aloud, I literally said, 'What the f*** are you doing with yourself?' before moving on.

I don't know why I said it or what part of me decided to say it, but it happened. That was the one question I seriously wanted to answer, but I never found the answer. I just hunkered down and worked as hard as I could but made no progress. I did that for years.

A few years later, I had an epiphany of sorts. I had worked as a surveyor for two years, and the company I was working for was terrible. Lousy customer service, slow turnarounds, a malicious boss, a toxic workplace, the works. So, I decided this was the new chapter I had been waiting for. I set out to start my own company. I had to burn bridges to leave, but I wasn't bothered. This was my turning point.

I was determined to make it work and gave it my all, more motivated than I had been in as long as I could remember. However, as the first year passed, I found myself in the surreal position where it seemed like the harder I worked at bringing my business to life, the less money I seemed to make and the more it seemed like it was failing. It didn't matter how much effort and time I put into things; my work wasn't generating any income. I was struggling to stay afloat.

And so, after many months of trying everything to heal my situation (that I could think of), I was at a loss - physically exhausted, sad and emotional, lethargic, and completely spent. Mortified, I had to ask friends and family for money. I had to work harder than I ever had before just to support myself, but I couldn't shake the feeling that it was all slipping through my fingers.

I had plans, and I knew what I needed to do. I had ideas for marketing and being more efficient, and I started to think about growing a team and setting all the foundations I knew I needed, but plans are just that.

Plans. They weren't my reality. Perhaps it was a case of trying at the wrong time in the wrong place.

Eventually, I drew the line and accepted that the business had failed. I couldn't keep asking family and friends to help keep me up and running. The guilt and the shame were too much. I was dead broke and deeply ashamed. The negativity, sadness, and despair came crashing down on me, and it felt like things would never change. I was back in this loop and no better off than I had been years before.

It all fell apart. I had to give up. There was no more fight left in me, and I no longer wanted to try. My dream had evaded me, and it was time to move on.

I know it sounds a bit dramatic, but it's the truth. If you've ever been in a similar position, you know how consuming it can be.

Unfortunately, as it tends to happen in situations like these, when it rains; it pours. You may have noticed that when bad things happen, they tend to be followed by an endless stream of other bad things. I'd given everything to make the business work and I was left with nothing.

I'd given up my home, car, money, and relationships. I was left with no more than a few personal belongings in a suitcase that I lugged around for an entire year. Twenty-five years old and couch surfing at friend's apartments, never staying more than a few days out of guilt and fear that I was burdening someone with my presence. It sounds dramatic, but that's genuinely how I felt.

This was my life. Trapped in a cycle of making a decision and feeling that it backfired every time. I would work so hard to save enough money to pull myself up to a place I could be proud of, but just a few weeks later, I would somehow be overdrawn with loan payments looming over me.

Of course, I *had* to do *something*. I was sick of this perpetual state of not knowing what I was doing. I was sick of not having any control over my life and seemingly wasting my hours just being pulled around by the currents of misfortune, thrown against the rocks every now and then.

Out of sheer desperation, I turned to the internet. As one does.

'You see,' I said to myself. 'Even if I don't know where to start or what to do, it's got to be better than this.'

And so, I started looking for answers. I needed

something. Maybe we're all just a product of our environment, and maybe this was the problem. So, I started thinking about changing my environment and doing things differently. I don't really know what I was thinking, but the first thing I did was go and sit in a local churchyard.

I thought that if we're all just made of atoms and energy, perhaps there was some kind of positive vibration or energy emanating from such a place. After all, people have been doing that for years through prayer. I was at a loss. At least if I went there, I might be able to feel some kind of energy that would help me out of the situation I was in. If I was lucky, maybe God would enlighten me and show me the way.

I figured that if sitting outside a churchyard was good enough for Einstein, it should be good enough for me. The only problem was that I couldn't really feel anything. A few sparrows were foraging for food on the ground, but that was about it. No spiritual awakenings stirred beneath the surface. No epiphany moments.

But then I started thinking about what else I could do to try and get myself out of the rut. I know I needed things. Material things. I needed money. I needed a stable job. I needed to figure out what to do about my abusive relationship and I certainly needed to work on my other relationships; whether that meant revitalizing old relationships or finding new ones.

Perhaps most importantly, I needed the confidence and courage to step out into the world and make all these things happen. For the last few years, I'd been trying to make things happen. I'd be trying to make my dreams come true and it had only left me worse off than when I started. My confidence and self-esteem was at an all-time low and that needed to change.

Hell, above all, I felt like I needed a drop of sanity or peace for once. But this raised very important questions. How could I bring all these things into my life? How could I attract them into my life?

Thinking about it in the moment, it all felt like so much that it may as well have been labeled impossible.

I got home later that evening and literally Googled 'how to attract stability,' and lo and behold, I saw articles about the Law of Attraction. At this point in my life, the Law of Attraction was a concept I'd heard of before but somehow had seemed to have forgotten about. I remember my mother had a copy of Rhonda Byrne's 'The Secret' on the bookshelf in the lounge of my childhood home. My grandmother used to talk about the Law of Attraction when I was younger too. She spent the first day of every new year creating vision boards to help her manifest her year, although I paid little attention to it at the time.

I also remembered watching an online self-help seminar about the Law of Attraction. Interesting, I thought to myself. Very interesting. It was as though pieces of a puzzle were starting to form in my mind, pulling at old memories I didn't even know I had. With no other solutions in mind, I pursued it. I started by getting educated.

At first, it made no sense at all. The idea that you could wish for something and simply get it seemed bizarre to me. But as I began to read more and learned about the law, I realized that it wasn't just a bunch of crap people liked talking about. It wasn't wishful thinking.

The Law of Attraction legitimately had real-world applications. The proof was everywhere and there are literally endless stories from people who have used the Law of Attraction to manifest their dream lives.

For example, motivational speakers like Tony Robbins talk about the Law of Attraction and apply its concepts in different ways, with statistics showing that he's reached the likes of over 50 million people. Celebrities like Will Smith and Jim Carrey regularly talk about their experiences of manifesting their desires using the same concepts and techniques we'll explore throughout this book.

Arnold Schwarzenegger is a popular example of someone who has used the Law of Attraction to achieve some powerful results. Known for being a gifted bodybuilder in his younger years, Arnold explained in plenty of interviews that he wanted to win the Mr. Universe title and this was his dream during this stage of his life. As a result, he used to envision and visualize his success by walking around ongoing tournaments like he was the top dog and had already won the title.

Arnold began his career at the age of 15 and ultimately went on to win the Mr. Universe title at the age of 20, which is an incredibly fast accomplishment given the competitiveness of the industry. What's more, he went on to win it six more times, and even though it's long since he stopped competing, his bodybuilding career has left a lasting legacy, and he remains one of the most famous bodybuilders in history.

There is even a US bodybuilding competition named The Arnold Sports Festival, which is considered the second-most important bodybuilding event in the world after Mr. Olympia.

Schwarzenegger was very proactive when it came to using the Law of Attraction, and the results have been incredibly clear throughout his career as a bodybuilder, a famous Hollywood actor, and even his political career as the Governor of the State of California. That's a lot of success for one man, but this is just one example of many people who have used the Law to beckon the universe to their side to manifest their dream life.

Jay-Z, Oprah Winfrey, Lady Gaga, Will Smith, and Denzel Washington all apply the Law of Attraction in their own lives and have spoken about it publicly. Even renowned UFC fighter Conor McGregor applies these teachings.

"If you can see it here (in your head), and you have enough courage to speak it, it will happen. I see these shots, I see these sequences, and I don't shy away from them. Often, people believe in certain things, but they keep to themselves. They don't put it out there. If you truly believe in it and become vocal with it, you are

creating that Law of Attraction, and it will become reality." - Conor McGregor, UFC 194.

When you consider that Law of Attraction books like 'The Secret' have sold over 35 million copies, and there are even references to the Law of Attraction in scriptures like The Bible, a text written over 3,000 years ago, it shows that this is something that has been a part of human culture for literally millenniums, and something worth looking into.

Of course, I was skeptical. But at the same time, for many years, I had watched as certain friends and family members got what they wanted. They were succeeding in making their dreams come true. They would ask for big things during casual conversations; a better career, more money, a new house or car, and I would watch in awe as their lives gradually changed over time. As hard as they may have worked to make it all happen (and believe me, they worked hard), without even knowing what it was that they were working towards, the things they wanted would eventually come into their lives.

And I could never understand why I seemed to miss out.

When I started out, I thought the Law of Attraction was

just an illusion, a way for people who couldn't hack it in the real world to make themselves feel better. A way for people who didn't know what they were doing with their lives to try and steer themselves in a more productive direction. I felt that it was one of those things that really only worked on TV, and while some people were lucky enough to fall into the right combination of good luck, good timing, and good karma (a perfect storm, so to speak), the vast majority of us had little hope when it came to making things happen. I believed we were stuck with our lot in life.

But then… I eventually changed my mind.

The Law of Attraction is not an illusion; it's a way for people to take control of their lives and steer it toward the things they want. The Law of Attraction does not mean that you sit back and expect others to bring the things you want into your life. Instead, it means that if you know what you're doing, you can take control of your destiny and make things happen.

What I found in my own journey is nothing short of incredible…

How the Law Of Attraction Works

What is the Law of Attraction? How does it work? How can you apply the Law of Attraction to your own life? Let's start with the basics.

The Law of Attraction. To get a basic understanding of

what this law entails, let's start with the science, and believe me, there is a *ton* of science supporting this.

Everything that exists in the universe has an energy vibration. Whether it's you, me, the building you're in, or the planet, they all have a vibration. This may sound a little complicated, especially if you're new to quantum physics, but the premise is really simple.

Scientists have determined that everything vibrates, even the atoms that make up matter. This means that everything is constantly in motion, not just the Earth orbiting the Sun at 67,000 miles per hour.

This is known as 'atomic vibration,' which is scientifically defined as the 'periodic motion of the atoms of a molecule relative.' Put simply - molecules and atoms will vibrate in relation to the molecules and atoms around them.

Interestingly, these same building blocks respond to energy. For example, if you heat water, you're transferring thermal energy into the water that doesn't just heat the water, but vibrates the atoms and electrons within the atoms.

This is how it works; if you focus your attention on something, your mind picks up its energy and sends it out into the universe. You then attract similar frequencies of vibration. You think of something that creates electrical signals or energy that expand out and vibrate other atoms. Let's take a look at a real-life example.

Let's say you want a new car. Day in and day out, all you can think about is your desire for that car; the color, style, leather interior, sound system, or speed... whatever it may be. You think about this car constantly, and these thoughts multiply to create a strong vibration. It becomes a powerful frequency of energy that is sent out to the universe and immediately attracts similar frequencies back to you.

And so, what happens? You get your new car! The law of attraction has brought it right to you.

In theory, at least! In reality, however, there is much more to it than that, but this is where you start.

The Law of Attraction is not just about asking for things; it's about feeling your desires with an intense passion and then letting go, knowing that the universe has got your message and will bring you what you desire when the time is right. It's no good sitting around day in and day out, thinking about how much you want something if you are not feeling it with every fiber of your being. The more you can feel what you want, the stronger your vibrational energy, and the easier it will be to manifest your desires.

If you just think, oh nice, yeah, I would love to have a million dollars, but you forget about it and don't feel it every day, it's never going to happen because vibrational energy isn't present.

It's the difference between wishing for things and knowing that you already have everything you need to make those wishes come true. There is no doubt about it; the Law of Attraction takes practice. It is not a magic trick that will work right away, but you can learn how to activate it at will with time and effort.

That's exactly what we're going to be covering in this book, and when I say it's going to be the last book you ever need, I mean it. We're going to explore everything about the science behind the practice and all the different ways you can start making it work for you.

So, let's begin with the theory.

CHAPTER TWO

The Science Behind the Law of Attraction

Everything is energy and that's all there is to it. Match the frequency of the reality you want and you cannot help but get that reality. It can be no other way. This is not philosophy. This is physics.
- Albert Einstein

Before you learn how to use the law of attraction consciously, it's important to know what is happening when you are using it unconsciously. After all, if you're not mindful of the energy you're sending out into the universe, you have very little control over the energy you're sending, and you're going to attract a lot of mess.

It's all about taking control, but first, you need to understand how it works. Now, let's build upon the foundation we laid in the first chapter.

The Law Of Attraction In Physics

According to physicists, our entire universe consists of vibrating strings of energy known as 'subatomic particles.' Because of this, it's said that our universe is one big 'vibration.' It's an endless vastness of vibrating subatomic particles, and everything in our physical reality, including human beings, is made up of them.

The way these energy vibrations behave determines the physical nature of the things around us, including how we feel, behave, and act. This is because our physical environment is not separate from us. In fact, what's around you right now is a reflection of how you're feeling.

Ever notice that when your mind is a mess, and you feel

like you're losing control, or bad things keep happening, the rest of your life starts to reflect this. Maybe your washing piles up, the dishes don't get cleaned, you end up not showering for days at a time, and your bedroom gets messier every day.

Your environment reflects your vibrations, and you have a lot of control over it. More than you think. That's because it's your space. Your vibrations interact and connect with the vibrations of our environments, surroundings, and other living beings.

Ever notice that if you're nervous around a dog, the dog will act nervous, anxious, or even defensive? Yet, if you're confident and caring, the dog will feel a lot more comfortable. This is an example of the interactivity of vibrational energy.

This doesn't just happen on a personal level. Science is literally founded on these ideas. For example, when hydrogen atoms are compressed together under the right conditions, they fuse and form helium (this process is known as nuclear fusion, emitting energy). When water molecules are heated to the boiling point, they evaporate into steam.

Interestingly, when scientists began studying the relationship between vibration and observable phenomena, they found that each note on a musical scale corresponds with a different type of particle vibrating at a different speed. It's important to note that the word 'note' could be replaced with the word 'frequency.'

The notes on a musical scale can be used to describe different types of human emotion. When we feel happy, it's like playing an A note. When we feel sad, it's like playing a D note. Use an online piano and try it for yourself, and you'll notice the shift in feelings (which is actually a shift in vibrational energy) almost instantly. This is where minor and major chords come into play.

In the same way that notes can be transposed into different frequencies when played on different instruments, human emotions can also be transformed by changing their frequency. The mind can change how we are feeling by changing its vibration. This is why we can feel happier, less stressed, and more positive simply by listening to uplifting music or watching something funny.

This is the transfer of different vibrational frequencies in full effect!

The Universe as a Vibrational Energy

All the atoms in our observable reality vibrate and resonate at different frequencies. The atoms that make up our planet, for instance, vibrate at a certain speed. The interactions between these vibrations give us 'observable events or phenomena' and create the different elements and forces in our physical world: gravity, electromagnetic radiation, and so on.

Even though they function separately, these atomic vibrations are all linked. Everything is interconnected and exert influence on everything in some form or another. This interdependence creates our reality. It's the fabric of reality that holds everything together. It's a mind-blowing concept, one that you can comprehend and not comprehend at the same time.

If you change the speed of a particle's vibration, you change its frequency. If you change a particle's frequency, you change its behavior and, therefore, your entire observable universe. If you change a particle's behavior, you change your physical reality.

This is how the universe works: When a group of atoms come together and resonate at the same frequency, they form 'particles' known as subatomic particles. These can be broken down even further into smaller oscillating frequencies of energy that vibrate whenever an electromagnetic wave comes into contact with it.

This is all there is to the universe: Vibrating particles of energy that make up a vibration or a frequency, and these frequencies can either be changed by resonance or harmonization (i.e., waves of electricity). Each of these frequencies creates a different type of particle, while each type of particle has a different atomic structure and frequency, which ultimately determines how these particles will interact with each other.

This may be hard to grasp since we perceive ourselves as many different things: people, animals, objects, etc., but in the grand scheme of things, all that exists is energy.

This brings us to a fundamental question: if we are just made up of energy, which creates different frequencies through different relationships, then what creates these relationships?

The answer is intention.

Intention (or thought) creates relationships and

interactions between frequencies. The more we focus on something, the clearer it becomes and the stronger the relationship between the two energies.

If you think about pink elephants all day, you'll start seeing pink elephants everywhere, even if there were none in sight before. A common example is when you're thinking about buying a new car. You may test drive a car, and for the next week, you'll see that car's make and model wherever you go.

This happens because you're so focused on something that your thoughts manifest it in the physical world around you. Everything that happens to you is created by your own mind. Your mind is your reality. What you perceive and think about is your world. If you don't think about it, don't see it, nor focus or perceive something, then it doesn't exist to you.

That doesn't mean it isn't physically there. It's like a stranger passing you in the street. If you don't know them and they don't mean anything to you, you don't notice or pay any attention to them. On the other hand, if they're your partner and you love them very much, you may only notice them and no one else. The reality for each person is different.

This reminds me of a time I went through a breakup. The energy of the breakup brought feelings like anger, sadness, loneliness, and separation, and these were the feelings I saw everywhere in the world around me. My entire world was filled with parents shouting at their children, other couples fighting, and sad movies.

Your thoughts and the energy of your thoughts manifest this reality to reflect your feelings. Boiling this idea down, only one universal law exists.

Like attracts like.

Sadness attracts sadness. Wealth attracts wealth. Peace attracts peace. Your mind and energy are reflected in your reality. Therefore, your mind creates your reality. What you put out is what you get back.

That's the law of attraction.

Here's the same logic as a formula:

Intention + Focus = Frequency (energy) Frequency → Attracts similar Frequency → Manifestation

Focus on what you want and spend very little time on what you don't want, and this energy will travel out into the universe to attract similar frequencies. The more thoughts you have of what you want, the stronger that frequency will become, and the faster and more firmly it will manifest in your physical world.

However, some other effects play into the Law of Attraction, and understanding these brings so much clarity to the table.

The Pygmalion Effect

The Pygmalion Effect is a social phenomenon where individuals raise their own performance standard to meet what they perceive to be the expected level of performance for someone in their position. This can be seen in many forms, whether it's athletes wanting to win because they think winning is what's expected of them or students studying harder because their parents expect more.

From an evolutionary standpoint, the Pygmalion Effect is a form of self-preservation. If you meet certain expectations, you'll be accepted by the rest of the community and you're more likely to survive.

To put this into a practical example, imagine you're a player on a football team. Since you're part of the team and you're practicing and getting better and better, mostly winning games and improving your skill as a player, you'll come to believe you're pretty good at the game. These are the expectations you have of yourself, or the expectations you believe other people have of you, i.e. your fans, your coach, your family and friends, your school or college, or the rest of your team.

The Pygmalion Effect can be a positive thing, and is generally considered this way from a professional standpoint. The high expectations can actually drive people to perform better because they're actively trying to match the expectations that are set for them. From the view of the Law of Attraction, this makes sense.

If you're surrounded by the vibrations that you're a winner and you're going to perform well and meet these high expectations, then you'll manifest a reality where you are actually performing at that expected level.

In your own life, you could set yourself the expectation that you're a good parent or you're a high performer at work, and so surrounding yourself with these vibrations causes you to live your life at that level. It's Law of Attraction 101.

However, you do have to be aware that this can work in the opposite way given the right circumstances.

However, there comes a match that matters, such as a championship final game, and you make a mistake that leads to you losing the game, such as missing the winning shot, missing a tackle, or fouling. This situation goes against all the expectations you had of yourself.

You thought you were great at what you did, but when push came to shove, you were unable to perform.

In a situation like this, it's almost impossible not to feel disappointed with yourself, and these are feelings that will linger and play on your mind. In a situation like this, the thoughts may play in your mind for weeks, months, or even years. If the thoughts become your way of thinking, your self-esteem and self-worth drops, and this becomes the energy you're putting out into the universe.

At the end of the day, there could be a million variables as to why your expectations weren't met, and many of them may not have even been your fault, but the situation happened and now you're left in this space, filled with negative, disappointed energy. Thus, the Law of Attraction starts working with this energy, and you'll enter a downward spiral.

Of course, this doesn't just apply to a sports player, but to anyone who has a job or a dream to make something happen. It could apply to your relationships, your family, or your individual health. We'll get into this a little more later, but it could even be something like going on a diet and then getting a take-out pizza that takes you down the same route of thinking.

The solution to the Pygmalion Effect is simple. If you want someone to perform better than they usually do, change your expectations by focusing on the times they have succeeded. Sure, this might not be enough to completely change your core expectations, especially if experience says you need to be careful, but it will give you something positive to focus on.

Just like the Law of Attraction, the Pygmalion Effect can be boiled down to the statement 'if you have a positive can-do attitude, then you'll have a positive outcome.'

The Golem Effect

Just like the Pygmalion Effect, the Golem Effect is a social phenomenon with a similar root concept: you attract what you think. The Golem Effect states that when an individual has negative thoughts or expectations about someone else's performance (or lack thereof), that person is likely to fail. Very similar, but not the same.

Whereas The Pygmalion Effect can be applied to thoughts about yourself or others, the Golem Effect refers to how you express your thoughts and how you affect the energy of others. For example, this is commonly seen in politics and debates where candidates try to convince the public that their opponent will not be able to handle something, such as being in office or handling a specific issue.

In other words, when people hear 'candidate A is not qualified for this position' enough times, they begin to expect candidate A's failure. This is the power of affirmations.

This is seen all the time in schools, colleges, and universities, in familial and romantic relationships, between friends, at the workplace, and so on. This is why most people love a good movie about an underdog. On a personal level, it's inspiring to see the main character defy expectations and succeed despite the negative energy they receive from everyone around them. Their belief in themselves far outweighs the negative, restricting vibrations from their environment.

Recently, I visited my uncle and auntie for a family Christmas dinner, and we found ourselves talking about health and diet. My uncle, who's diabetic, is trying to lose weight, and both my auntie and uncle were bickering about how they've tried to change their diet.

'I will. I will lose a stone by the end of next year,' my uncle exclaimed adamantly.

'No, you won't, you said this last year, and you've put on weight. I don't believe it,' my auntie responded.

'No, I will. You watch.'

It was an interesting conversation to watch. There are two opposing forces at work, and it's down to whose belief will manifest the desired reality. If my uncle listens to my auntie and takes in the vibrational energy she's sending into the universe, he won't lose weight.

On the other hand, if he believes in himself strongly enough, through the power of the Law of Attraction, as we'll go through later in this very book, he will succeed. This is the kind of power we're working with.

With these effects in mind and a more solid understanding of the Law of Attraction, we can see that energy attracts similar energy. That's the foundation of this process. The energy you put out into the world through your thoughts, your actions, and your decisions is the energy you'll get back, and once you understand this, you can start taking control.

This means controlling the energy you're putting out, therefore controlling the energy you're getting back. It's about being intentional with your life. You'll start seeing opportunities you would not have seen before, things that can help you get what you want.

CHAPTER THREE

Defining the Seven Laws of Attraction

You create your thoughts, your thoughts create your intentions, and your intentions create your reality.
- Wayne Dyer

The ability to synchronize your mind with the universe to attract what you want is a powerful skill, but it's impossible to put into practice if you're unaware of how it works.

While there are hundreds of books written on this

subject, it's important to note that there are only seven core laws of attraction. These laws act as a foundation for everything else. Created through years of study and research in quantum mechanics, psychology, metaphysics, and other disciplines, these are essential in creating a solid foundation upon which the rest of your knowledge can be built.

Law #1 - The Law of Manifestation

To be conscious is a choice. It's a choice to bring your awareness mindfully into the present moment, giving you the unique opportunity to see what is happening and therefore prioritizing what you focus on and the direction you take your life.

The Law of Manifestation is founded on the concept that all manifested reality in the universe begins with a thought. This could be a conscious thought or an unconscious thought that loops in your mind, sometimes without your realization.

Regardless of its origins, your thought has the potential to manifest in your life via the Law of Attraction.

Everything you see in your life started off as an idea, and

here's a simple example to prove it.

How would you go about manifesting an apple?

First, you need to decide that you desire an apple. In this example, choosing a delicious red apple instead of a green one doesn't matter because, in reality, the 'appleness' is not what decides whether it can become real or not. You've just decided that you want one.

So, you've had this initial thought, thus sending that energy out into the world. With that, you begin a three-step process

The first step involves having a clear idea about what you want. Without being 100% clear on what you want, you're not going to be able to send out the vibrations needed to manifest it. The clearer you can be with your goal, the more accurately you'll be able to bring it into existence.

The second step involves having a clear vision or idea of where and how you want to see this apple appear. If the first step is the what, the second step is all about the when and the how.

You have to think about what dimensions it exists in — is it an image on your computer screen, an actual apple that you can touch and hold, or an apple that exists in your imagination? This process further defines your desire and will help more accurate manifestations.

Bring clarity to your desire. This is where the power of visualization comes into play, and the more defined you can be with what you want, the more the Law of Attraction will work in your favor.

We'll get into this a little more later, but for now, focus on your senses. Focus on as much detail as possible. What does it feel like? What does it taste like? Where is it going to come from?

The third step involves believing that your thoughts can become real. You need to truly believe that what you're seeing has the potential to be real. If you spend all this time and energy thinking about manifesting an apple in your life, but then tell yourself, 'Ah, what's the point? It's never going to happen.' Of course, it's never going to happen because your thought is now overriding your desire for an apple.

This is the Law of Manifestation.

Law #2 - The Law of Pure Desire

The Law of Pure Desire states that you attract into your

life whatever you focus on intensely, whether those thoughts are positive or negative. Positively, this means that if you remain committed to something long enough, you will see it manifest in your life. Negatively, this means that if you continually obsess about something or someone, you will also see it manifest in your life, for better or for worse.

For the Law of Attraction to work for you, you need to have a pure desire for what you want to manifest. This means that if you're aiming for something you don't really want or believe in, then it's not going to manifest. You simply don't want it strongly enough.

This is where many people misunderstand the Law of Pure Desire. They believe attraction is only possible if their goal is grand and overwhelming enough to command all their thoughts. Think of goals like New Year's Resolutions, where people hope that they can introduce a new angle to their life that will change their lives forever.

The problem with this is that goals like this tend to be large and general. They're not specific enough for the individual to clearly see how to achieve them or what small steps need to be taken daily.

As a result, they continuously plan for their goal without

taking any real action. Having a broad goal is just a wish. A fantasy. A dream. It's not powerful enough to inspire any action, so the want never manifests.

Pure desire means not only wanting something, but wanting and needing that desire more than anything. If you want something so badly but then you think, 'Oh, my parents won't want me to go down that path?' or 'Oh, I don't think I'll have enough money to see that idea through,' you're making excuses and therefore it won't manifest.

You need to desire what you want purely, so much so that nothing will stand in your way. Nothing will hold you back. You may think of excuses, but they are quickly dismissed because you know in your soul that you'll find a way to make it work, whatever the cost. You have no fear seeking out these desires and no fear living in a reality where that exists.

You believe you are worthy of what you want and that you deserve what you desire. This is the Law of Pure Desire.

The Law of Delicate Balance

The Law of Delicate Balance is one of the foundational

laws that often goes unacknowledged. This law states that you will get back what you put in – no more and no less. It's the Yin and Yang of the law of attraction. There must always be balance with everything in life, even if it takes time for it to manifest.

It's a law that ensures that you're capable of sustainably manifesting your goals, that you can remain grounded, and that you are capable of living your life properly.

To make this clear, let's imagine you're focusing your attention on manifesting your dream career. An example would be undertaking the pursuit to manifest your dream career.

Once the idea to pursue your dream is there, you can start making it happen. In this case, it means working hard and making the right decisions, taking professional opportunities when they come your way at the right time. However, sacrifices will need to be made at some point.

However, during this period of working hard, it can become so easy for other areas of your life to fall out of balance in pursuit of this end goal, and to cut a long story short, the Law of Delicate Balance helps ensure that you don't end up spiraling and losing everything.

For example, you could start working long hours at the office, but you sacrifice other important aspects of your life, such as by not eating, sleeping, socializing, or exercising properly.

Over time, you'll start feeling unhealthy, lonely, and at risk of developing mental health issues. Because of this negative energy, your original goal ends up being pushed away further from you because you're attracting all these negative things. For example, if you're working hard and you're constantly telling yourself 'Oh my, I'm so tired and burned out all the time,' this is what you'll manifest, and your original dream of fulfilling a career goal will drift away as you begin to resent how you're living your life.

The Law of Delicate Balance ensures that your desires are fulfilled at the right time, naturally, without extra effort on your part. In this case, if you need to learn how to look after yourself and balance both work and play, this law will ensure you won't reach this goal until you're able to do this successfully.

The Law of Attraction works within you, and it won't allow you to fulfill your end goal only for you to throw it away because you haven't got the skills or abilities to sustain it.

The Law of Magnetism

The Law of Magnetism states that people, events, and situations are drawn to you by your thoughts. Thoughts that resonate with what you want to manifest will be amplified in lieu of this law, while those which don't resonate will be pushed aside from your reality.

For example, if you want to meet someone who makes you laugh, this will be amplified by the Law of Magnetism and will cause situations in your reality where people make you laugh (or at least try to).

This is why it's important to focus on what's great in your life because this will make you feel better, and it'll allow you to attract even more great things into your life.

Specific laws govern the physical world, just as mental laws govern our thoughts. The Law of Magnetism deals with things coming into your life that appear to happen by chance or coincidence. This includes people you have never met before offering to help you, opportunities appearing seemingly out of nowhere, and seemingly random events that change your life.

There are no accidents in the Universe, and everything is connected. This includes your connection to other people who are thousands of miles away, complete strangers. You can never tell where or when a person will show up in your life - it could be through the Law of Magnetism, even if it seems coincidental.

The Law of Magnetism allows you to see all the pieces come together as events, people and experiences flow into your life to bring you better luck than you ever thought possible. You can follow this principle to find those opportunities where money is involved, but do not stop there.

Many people focus on the money they seek, but the Law of Magnetism can bring more than just dollars and cents into your life. You can also see your health improve through this law. It is all connected - the better your health is, the better your life is. A healthy body generates a healthy mind which attracts positive people and circumstances into your life.

If you have had a run of bad luck, the Law of Magnetism can help you figure out why this is happening. When you can identify what is causing your problems, it becomes much easier to fix them.

The Law of Abundance

While the Law of Delicate Balance says that you'll get what you put in (no more and no less) and that all areas of your life must have balance, the Law of Abundance states that you will always have enough, regardless of what you're striving for, and that there is more than enough for everyone.

If you decide that you want to have a house by the sea, the law of abundance ensures you still have all of your needs met, even if you don't have a house by the sea yet. Most people interpret this to mean that they should just be satisfied with what they already have, but that's not quite true.

This is important because you may make excuses not to do things in your life. You might say you can't write a bestselling book because so many other people are doing it. You can't become an athlete because there are people faster than you. You can't get that promotion since so many of your colleagues are already going for it.

Affirmation-wise, if you say statements like this, statements like 'I can't get that promotion,' then you won't because this is the energy you're putting out, and the Law of Attraction will act accordingly. However, you can ensure you don't feed yourself these statements by trusting the Law of Abundance, which ensures that there's more than enough success, money, fame, love, peace, happiness, and so on to go around.

Just because someone else has it doesn't mean there's less for you, but if you believe that there's not enough, then this is the reality you'll manifest.

This is a brilliant law for making sure that you don't get stuck in the mindset of saying, 'Hey, everyone else is successful, so they have it, and I can't.' We all have access to everything we want, our own forms of success in our own way. It's all about reaching out to take it rather than blaming our lack on anybody else.

The Law of Expanding Influence

Isn't it true that everyone could use a little more kindness in their lives? This idea epitomizes this sentiment. The Butterfly Effect is related to the Law of Expanding Influence, except it is more applicable to benevolence.

The Law of Expanding Influence's primary premise is that a simple act of kindness performed by one person can impact hundreds of others down the chain of contact. It's the notion that their act of kindness can have an enormous impact.

Let me give you an example. Let's imagine a woman is walking down the street and comes into contact with another woman dressed in a stunning gown. She compliments the woman's beautiful gown, putting her in a better mood. She treats her boss with a little more kindness now that she's in a better mood, and he, in turn, treats his employees better.

Employees are in a better mood, and they are gentler to their families when they go home. The woman's innocuous remark has now influenced dozens of individuals! Imagine she compliments five more individuals that day, spreading the kindness even further! This is a chain reaction, or butterfly effect.

The opposite also holds true. Consider the following scenario: It's a rainy day, and a man has forgotten his umbrella, so as he boards the bus, he belittles the bus driver. The driver is now in a foul mood, and everyone who boards or exits the bus is treated with a little less courtesy. Everyone he comes into contact with is now in a bad mood or, at the very least, doesn't feel as kind. They go out into the world and disseminate that negativity, and the cycle continues until someone breaks the chain, allowing a more positive image to be projected onto others.

I'm not suggesting that if someone hands you something a little more complicated than usual it will harm mankind, but it certainly won't help mankind. And who knows, maybe that melancholy snowballs into something bigger than a bad mood. What if it contributes to family violence or teaches a youngster a terrible lesson? Humans are impressionable, and we are more influenced by those around us than we may realize. Because the world could always use a little more kindness, all I'm suggesting is to be kind. You never know the impact it can have on someone.

The Law of Synchronization

The Law Of Synchronization states you will attract things, events, and people in your life who are in resonance with the vibrations you have within. It means the vibrations you have within you and those you emit to the universe will attract those that are synchronized to those frequencies. This is just building off what I've covered, the premise that like attracts like. This is the law that makes that happen.

For example, if you feel happy, confident, and enthusiastic, your vibration will sync with these feelings and attract situations with similar feelings. As a result, your experiences will be more fulfilling and enjoyable, and you'll find yourself connecting to others who feel the same.

You could, in theory, try to ignore how you feel, but this could, in turn, cause you to block what you want to manifest. For example, let's say you're angry with your boss, but pretend that everything is fine and you ignore your feelings because you want to continue to work hard to fulfill your dreams of becoming successful in your career.

However, feeling angry towards your boss may be a sign to find another job, and it's in this new place of work that you end up being successful in your career. To ignore your feelings is to ignore the path you were meant to take, thus preventing the manifestation of your success.

If you listen to your subconscious mind, accept your feelings and emotions, and stay present, you can tune into how you really feel, following your path to ultimately manifest what you desire.

Nature is a prime example of balance. Nature has perfect synchronization - every living thing gets up at dawn, goes to sleep at dusk, replaced by nocturnal animals. Plants and animals grow and reproduce at certain intervals, all synchronized with each other.

The winds at the Equator, for example, carry the dust from the Sahara Desert to the Amazon jungles of South America, fertilizing the ground for new plant life to grow. On a global scale, the planet is balanced. Even comets and asteroids that have crashed into the Earth over the last millions of years contained minerals that make up our planet today. The universe is in balance.

One of the best things you can is to look out for signs and the connections around you. Look out for Synchronization taking place in your day-to-day life. The best way to do this is to increase your awareness of your surroundings. The more aware you are, the easier it will be for you to find what you want in life because everything is interconnected - like a big puzzle or game that we are all trying to solve.

When you realize that everything is a part of you, you start to understand why things happen. You will also see how easily your thoughts and feelings affect the world around you. It is also important to know that every living thing carries its own individual frequency - a unique set of vibrations.

Think of a radio station and how it broadcasts at a certain frequency. You can tune into this frequency or not. This is what happens when people 'tune in' to your frequency - they receive your signal. When they pick up on your frequency, you become part of their lives.

The Law of Conscientious Action

The Law of Conscientious Action states that 'we attract into our lives what we are committed to creating.' This complements the other laws, specifically the Law of Pure Desire.

People tend to apply this law to their personal growth and development, but it can be applied to anything. If you desire something new in your life - whether it's a new house or car, healthy relationships, better finances, more prestige at work, etc. - what you are committed to creating determines whether or not you will have it in your life.

You cannot attract something you are not committed to creating into your life. If you really want something, you need to be 100% committed to creating it in your life, 100% committed to taking action, and 100% dedicated to seeing it through. This is why in the previous law, I mentioned not ignoring how you feel.

If you're angry at your boss and want to leave your job, this is the path you need to take to succeed in your career. But this law maintains that you need to be committed to making that happen.

When you are not committed and you cannot manifest what you want, you'll get frustrated and believe that the Law of Attraction is a crock. However, what's really happening is that you did not want it enough and weren't committed to manifesting it, so the Law of Attraction manifested your lack of commitment.

This begs the question; what determines commitment?

The more emotionally attached you are to something, the more committed you are to it. When you attach emotion to something, you're saying that it's important enough to warrant an emotional response from you, requiring a stronger level of commitment on your part.

For example, you might want to become a photographer, and you decide that you need a DSLR camera to get started. However, these new cameras are several hundred dollars each, and it's a bit of a large investment. You might have a few ideas of models you want for a good price, but then decide to get some new computer games instead, or that you want to get a new car.

Because you're making decisions to buy other things, you're not taking Conscientious Action towards your goal, and therefore, your dreams of being a photographer are not going to manifest. You could try and find a pre-owned camera, but if you're not thinking about these options, you're not taking action, and nothing will manifest.

Another example could be wanting a new house. You visit a few homes but they all have things wrong with them and you're always finding excuses in small ways. Perhaps you see a house that needs a little cosmetic work before it's ready to move into, and you feel discouraged and begin to consider other options. When this happens, your emotional attachment to the house isn't enough, so you won't commit and make a purchase.

On the other hand, if you are committed, it shows with the energy you put out into the universe. You want a new car so badly that your emotions drive everything about it - how it looks, how fast it goes, the color, the type of fuel it uses, etc. When you attach this level of emotion to anything in your life, you're 100% committed to creating that thing.

The more emotionally attached you are to something, the more potent your commitment is to have it in your life. It's this commitment that will drive you to make the conscious action that will manifest what you desire.

This is an important part of the Law of Attraction, and being able to master it will enable you to do so much. Of course, you need to be able to increase your emotional attachment to the things you want, which is precisely what you'll do with some of the strategies I've discussed, like visualization and affirmations, plus some of the other strategies explored in the later chapters.

By combining all these laws together, you should have a clear idea of what elements go into the umbrella term that is the Law of Attraction, how the elements work, and how switching what you're focusing on can change everything you want to change and give you complete control over the direction of your life.

CHAPTER FOUR

Explaining the Vibrations

"Your personal vibration or energy state is a blend of the contracted or expanded frequencies of your body emotions and thoughts at any given moment. The more you allow your soul to shine through you, the higher your personal vibration will be."

- Penney Peirce

I've repeatedly referenced 'vibrations' in the previous sections, but now it is time to focus on how important vibrations are in the manifestation process. After this chapter, we're going to get into the actionable part of taking control and having the Law of Attraction work for you, so let's first explore what vibrations are.

How Do Vibrations Work with the Law of Attraction?

Every thought contains a certain vibration. Thoughts containing higher frequencies are easier to manifest, while those with lower frequencies will not be as effective. Your thoughts dictate how you feel, and everything that's happening around you is as a result of what you feel at any given moment. The stronger those thoughts or, the more consuming they are, the higher the vibration, and the higher the chance of that thought manifesting.

The problem is that so many people have been brainwashed to believe that life is supposed to be difficult. Yes, life is complicated, and there's a lot going on. Life isn't without problems or bad times, but your reality depends on your perspective.

There's a very famous Chinese short story that goes something like this.

There was a farmer and one day his horse ran away. The village people said it was a sad moment, but the farmer replied, maybe. The next day, the horse returned with seven wild horses, and so the farmer now had eight horses. The villagers said how amazing this was, but the farmer said maybe.

The next day, the farmer's son was working with the new horses, and one horse was suddenly startled, lashing out and kicking the boy, ultimately breaking his leg. The boy then had to stay in the house to recover. The villagers said how awful that was, but the farmer still replied 'maybe.'

Soldiers came to the village to draft the boys and men for the ongoing war the following day. They passed by the farmer's house and saw the boy with the broken leg, meaning he couldn't be drafted and had to stay at home instead of going to war. The villagers stated how amazing this was. The farmer said maybe.

The moral of this story is that seemingly good and bad things will happen to you throughout your life, but you can never really tell if they're good or bad. You might lose your job and feel like it's the worst thing to happen to you, but if you end up in a job you love a few weeks later, then it was a good thing.

This is how you need to start looking at all aspects of your life.

Many people feel there's a lot of negativity in the world, and because of this, their minds are programmed to notice things that support this point of view. I've done it. I've been there, and I know lots of people who have. We see it every single day.

Using the media as an example, we're all told about all the doom and gloom in the world, and thus we are conditioned to look for it since it's what everyone else seems to be focused on. Moreover, due to the way humans have evolved, looking for the negative is a survival tactic.

We are instinctually on the lookout for danger and things that may harm us so we can protect ourselves from them. Because we live in a hyper-connected world, we hear all the bad things happening around the world all the time.

On a more personal level, the conditioned beliefs you

developed while growing up, through parents, friends, and your own personal experiences, influence your perspective and how you perceive the negative aspects of the world.

If you're on the lookout for the negatives in the world, this becomes your vibrational frequency, and you'll manifest negativity. Like attracts like. The energy you put out into the universe is the energy you'll get back.

I've experienced this personally many times throughout my life. I remember being really toxic to another girl at work. I was having a bad day and was abnormally mean to her when she knocked something off my desk. It wasn't a big deal, and there's no excuse for it; it's just what I did, and I was being mindless at the time.

The next day, I met up with a new client and they were so rude and horrible, but it was a necessary contract, so I had to sit and deal with it. A day later, I apologized to the girl and set the record straight, and I was moved to a new contract with a much nicer client. This was all before I knew about the Law of Attraction, but it's a shining example of how like attracts like.

Imagine you miss the bus or train to work and end up running late. You might end up walking to work bitter about the experience, playing over the conversations you're going to have with your boss and coworkers, practicing excuses, figuring out how to move your deadlines or cope with your growing workload, and other similar hypothetical situations.

The more negative energy you're putting out mindlessly by focusing on the negative things in life, the more negativity you'll have in your life.

However, it's not all about negative energy, as the same logic very much applies to positive vibrations as well! If you go for a night out with friends, the vibrations can be so positive when you're all out for the same reason that you all bounce off each other and end up having nights you'll never forget that are just so much fun and so carefree. Those times in your life where you're just surrounded by amazing people and you're all 'vibing' together, all happen because you're all on the same vibration.

This is surely the case when you go to a wedding and everything is having fun while celebrating love, or when you go to a concert, gig, or festival, and the entire atmosphere is just so incredibly electric, you can feel it pulsing within you. That's due to the fact there's such a high density of positive vibrations around you that you can't help but align with it. That's what happens when so many people on the same frequency get together, especially when there's music involved which literally sends frequencies out into the universe.

When it comes to positive and negative vibrations, the very best thing you can do is tune into your thoughts and define what kind of vibrations they're sending out.

Personally, I found it so difficult to not only know whether what I was thinking was positive or negative, but I didn't really have any clue as to what I was thinking at. Every day was just a big continuous blur where it seemed as though my thoughts just came and went so quickly, I was never in a constant state of mind.

It wasn't until I took the time to journal and take actual notice of my thoughts - processing them and writing them down - that I was able to see exactly what I was thinking throughout the day and whether or not I was putting positive or negative vibrations out into the world.

This is why it's so important to record your thoughts every day so that you can get a clear picture of what's going on in your mind. If you can identify the thoughts that are playing over and over again in your head, then you can see what kind of energy you're putting out into the world.

So, when negative thoughts are recorded, find a way to raise their vibration. Otherwise, you won't make positive changes in your life. Likewise, make sure to record the positive thoughts as well, focusing on the things you want and the things that matter to you, so you can actually see where your mind is at.

Let's take a deep dive into this.

Positive Vibrations

The Law of Attraction states that positive vibrations attract positivity. It's important to remember this if you want the Law of Attraction to work for you.

So how can you make sure that your positive vibrations are strong enough?

One way is to surround yourself with things and people who will likely influence you positively. There will be plenty of things you are emotionally tied to. You might have a favorite song or place that takes you back to a first date when you were happy. You may have a favorite movie. You might have an object that reminds you of a place or a gift that a loved one gave you.

Whatever it is, these things are the best options for increasing your positivity. You can also use the process of gratitude to increase your positive vibrations, which is, fortunately, one of the simplest methods available. You can also try meditating to get rid of negative thoughts and feelings, which will strongly affect your vibrations.

It's these positive vibrations that will help you bring success to your life, and not just financial or career-based success. What I mean is that these vibrations will help you attract people who will make your life better and provide you with things that are necessary for you to be truly happy.

If you can continue to channel positive vibrations throughout all areas of your life or raise your negative vibrations, you'll be able to change your life in unbelievable ways. Physically, you'll feel better and therefore take better care of yourself, eat healthier food and get more exercise, and mentally you'll experience the joys of success and happiness. You'll feel more peaceful, sleep better, and experience less stress in all areas of your life.

When you start focusing on what's good in your life, rather than constantly seeking out what's wrong, life really starts to work in your favor.

What are Negative Vibrations?

Of course, we also experience negative vibrations since the universe requires balance. They have to exist. However, negative vibrations aren't necessarily a bad thing. Using my previous example, you might lose your job and feel sad about it. Perhaps you may even be scared since you're uncertain about what your future holds.

These feelings are understandable, but they embody negative vibrations. If you constantly focus on these vibrations and continuously tell yourself that you're scared about what your future holds, you'll stay in a state of anxiety. However, these vibrations aren't necessarily a bad thing since they can motivate, inspire, and push you to make a positive change in your life, turning the negative vibrations into positive ones. That's the balance. Negative vibrations become problematic when they consume your life or at least some aspects of it, as is the case for so many people.

Negative vibrations are so easy to find today because of

our access to vast sources of information. The internet has made it possible for people to put their negative thoughts out into the universe, even if they don't know anyone who shares them or who will contact them.

If you go on Twitter to complain about something, the action of writing or reading a negative Tweet or comment propels negative energy into the universe, affirming whatever it is you're writing about, making the statement your reality. The more you affirm these thoughts, the more concretely they become your reality, and you'll find yourself getting deeper and deeper into the rut of living with negative vibrations. The more energy you feed these vibrations, the more prevalent they'll become.

The media, specifically the news, is a major source of negativity because the focus is mainly on the bad news. Media sources - especially ones that focus on drama, gossip, speculative stories, and negative stories - send a ton of negative energy out into the world.

This energy connects with people harboring that same energy, perpetuating it. This is because other people feel this energy, which triggers them to be negative.

You've probably felt the negativity the media emits, especially if you read the news or watch the TV often.

But, the media and the internet aren't the only sources of negative energy. People living with negative vibrations will pass them on to you if you maintain contact with them.

If you're in a toxic relationship with an abusive partner, their energy can cause the negative energy in you to fester. If you're in a toxic workplace where people are horrible to each other and burnout is prevalent, this environment will affect your own energy fields. Places in your life, such as a church where a loved one is buried, or an object, like a gift from a toxic friend, can also harbor negative energy that can affect you if you let them.

Everyone is sending out energy, either positive or negative, through their thoughts, words, and actions. This is the Law of Attraction at work because what you focus on is what you'll manifest. You can't send out positive vibes if that's not what you're thinking about. The same goes for negative energy.

If you're not aware of your negative energy and you're relatively mindless with it, then you won't be able to do anything about it. To master the balance of vibrations, you need to focus on affirming the positive vibrations in your life (at least the ones you want to work with), acknowledging the negative ones, and using them as your foundation for change.

It's not easy. You may have negative thoughts that have been festering for years, unconsciously. I recently noticed that I've been harboring a lot of negativity about my weight. I'm continuously telling myself I'm not happy with my weight and that I'm getting overweight, which just continues that train of thought. The language I'm using to describe my weight affirms it, thus the law of attraction ensures I am what I believe.

Negative thoughts are often so strong because people have been conditioned into thinking that it's how they should feel about certain things. For example, many people believe that they should hate their jobs rather than simply not liking some aspects of the job. If you work somewhere where everyone has a toxic mindset, low vibrations will thrive, and everyone will be miserable, attracting more negativity into other areas of their lives.

The takeaway here is that you should keep your mind open to identifying where negative energy is in your life, and instead of letting that become your primary focus - giving it more of your time or energy, or surrounding yourself with it - take note of it and reframe your mind to develop a positive and affirming outcome.

For example, instead of just getting up and going to work every day and telling yourself that you hate it, break it down and highlight the actual areas that are bothering you.

Do you hate your boss? Your coworkers? Do you not have enough responsibilities? Is your work meaningful or satisfying? Are you in a career you want to be in? Are you being paid enough for what you do? Find the area of your life that holds negative energy, and simultaneously, look for areas of your job that bring positive vibrations into your life.

This process of identifying your thoughts and breaking them down, then redefining your focus to what you want it to be, is the foundation for mastering the Law of Attraction.

So, look inside yourself, and see what your thoughts are. Write them down and brainstorm ideas. Some sources of negative vibrations may be straightforward. Maybe you think negatively about your body image, finances, or relationships. Maybe you spend a lot of time online consuming sources of information that promote negative vibrations.

In some cases, you may generate negative vibrations internally and through your actions, such as engaging in gossip or worrying about something that hasn't happened yet. You may have some traumas you need to heal, or you may feel angry, bitter, or jealous towards other things in life, all of which are powerful ways to lower your vibrations.

Taking the time to go through this process is important because so many people are unaware of how their negative thoughts and feelings affect them and how devastating their impact can be. Negative thoughts contribute to both tangible and intangible manifestations, such as poor health, business failures, toxic relationships, and mental health issues.

Negative vibrations affect both your physical and mental health. This is backed by science. Your mind and body are inextricably linked, so it's far from surprising that a bad mood can cause physical problems, such as aches, pains, trouble sleeping, headaches, and so on. This is why we typically fall ill when we're stressed or when we're sad. The body reflects the mind.

If you ever reach a point in your life where you feel as though you have nothing good in your life and everything is chaotic, it's because you've continuously onboarded negative energy in all aspects of your life. This has continuously lowered your vibrations over time, and because like attracts like, you only attract more negative energy. Thus, you stay in the rut and seemingly never-ending downward spiral.

Scientifically, there's a clear difference between positive and negative energy.

For example, there's a difference between powering yourself and depleting yourself. Powering yourself using positive energy is like charging your battery, while depleting yourself using negative energy is like draining your battery. If you drain all your power, you become exhausted, unable to do anything. It's far easier to get what you want when you have a strong power source, so make sure to keep your battery full!

Additionally, when you're in this negative, drained, and exhausted state of mind, it's much harder for you to notice the good things happening in your life. Being happy and positive will be a daunting task, and you'll miss out on opportunities and choices because you won't be in a position to notice them.

Understanding how vibrations work is essential if you want to make the most out of the Law of Attraction.

CHAPTER FIVE

Deliberate Attraction

"Like the air you breathe, abundance in all things is available to you. Your life will simply be as good as you allow it to be."
- Abraham Hicks

Deliberate attraction is a term used to describe the idea of correctly applying the Law of Attraction in your life. Reading about the law of attraction is essential, but if you want to harness its power and start moving your life in the direction you want, you need to be deliberate with your thoughts and actions.

The truth is that the Law of Attraction is constantly affecting your life. The energy you put out into the universe is the energy you get back, whether you're intentionally doing this or not. If you're mindlessly going through life, the energy you attract will fluctuate dramatically. If you are deliberate with what you're sending out into the universe, you become more deliberate with the energy you're getting back and your vibrational frequency.

Imagine you're not happy with your job, and you're trying to do something about it - earning more money, getting a promotion, finding a job you can be happy with, dealing with co-workers, managers, and so on. Whatever the problem is, you're trying to find a way out and into a new state of mind.

As I mentioned earlier, there are a few reasons why you might not be getting what you want from the Law of Attraction. This may be because you don't fully understand it, or you could be subconsciously blocking your good fortune with your thoughts.

Let's say you're working on a project and you're finding your co-workers really irritating because they're not pulling their weight. This could leave you feeling bitter and under pressure to do more because you want the project to go well. However, this bitterness towards your co-workers is causing you to send out bitter, resentful vibrations out to the universe, thus you're going to quickly find yourself with a bitter and resentful end result.

Another example could be that you're struggling with money. You're trying to find enough money to pay your bills and have some savings and live your life, but how you move forward will depend on the vibrations you're sending out. For example, if you're saying something like 'I have no money and I'm so screwed all the time,' then this is the energy you're putting out into the universe, and you'll end up in a loop where this keeps happening.

This is exactly what happened to me. When my business was failing, I kept saying to myself how badly I needed to get money and how poor my financial situation was, and due to my phrasing, I remained in that position.

Once I'd taken steps to focus on my phrasing and take control of my vibrations, such as working on my thought process and rephasing my concerns to statements like, 'I am in control of my financial situation and I am learning and bettering myself,' real change started to happen.

Your subconscious mind is very powerful. It's like a magnet; it's able to attract the right things even if you don't realize it. You can see this when people say that they've been attracting the same kind of partner over and over again, but they're not happy with them. It's because they've subconsciously attracted this type of person through their negative vibrations, and until they notice that there is a problem, they will continue to appear in their lives.

When your feelings are right, and you're focusing on what you want in life with positive intentions, the Law of Attraction begins working for you, not against you. It's important to remember how powerful and rewarding the Law of Attraction can be when we learn to master it and take responsibility for our thoughts, feelings, and emotions. Once you start being deliberate with your thoughts and deliberately attracting what you want, you'll become your own proof, and you can continue to attract based on the momentum you build.

I can go into extreme detail about my own life and how the law of attraction has worked for me, as many people - public speakers, philosophers, authors, and so on - have, but this will only get you so far.

I was able to build my self-worth and self-esteem from the ground up using the power of affirmations, which embraces the use of words to create positive vibrations. Back when my business failed and I was well and truly stuck in a rut, I was at an all-time low, and crashing on friends' sofas while I had no money was hard. It was embarrassing and I couldn't shake the feeling that I was a failure. I felt I was incapable, and nothing was going my way.

Of course, my self-confidence and self-worth hit rock bottom, and I was stuck in that continuous cycle because I was manifesting so much negativity with my thoughts and feelings of no self-worth. However, as I started out my journey of mastering the power of the Law of Attraction, I found there were so many ways to turn my thinking around.

For example, even an act as simple as looking in the mirror and telling myself that I was going to have such an amazing day literally manifested amazing days. Instead of being wrapped up in my thoughts, I was taking the time to put positive vibrations out into the universe, thus they were coming back to me.

Mel Robbins, life coach and modern-day motivational speaker, recently released a new, science-backed technique where you wake up and go to the mirror, set an intention for what kind of day you want, and then give yourself a high-five in the mirror. Yes, it can feel a little silly if you're doing this for the first time.

I tried it myself, and it works. It works every day. But this is what I mean by it's so easy to just say what's happened to me. I can tell you my journey, and it's evident since you're holding my book in your hands, but it doesn't really hit home just how powerful this stuff is until you're experiencing it for yourself.

However, it's up to you to put these actions into practice.Once you start experiencing it for yourself, then you can really start to feel the benefits, and since your vibrations are already high, you'll keep going because you'll have become your own proof that it works.

Now, that brings us to what could be the most important section of this book. Now that we've pretty much covered all the theories you need to know, it's time to dive into the practical aspects of the Law of Attraction. Of course, we've covered some basics, but now it's time to master what you know to deliver real results.

It's time to start deliberately applying the rules of the Law of Attraction to really see what it's capable of.

Harnessing the Power of Deliberate Attraction

There are several different ways to harness the power of deliberate attraction. You've already learned about some of them in this book, such as shifting your thoughts and feelings, using affirmations, visualization, and taking the time to identify your thoughts in all areas of your life, but how do you actually do this?

All these strategies work because they help you control your thoughts, feelings, and emotions, and help you attain deliberate focus on what you want. As I mentioned earlier, there's an unlimited amount of power behind the Law of Attraction. All you need to do is harness it to start getting what you want out of life.

It's important to realize how powerful deliberate attraction can be when used correctly. Like most things in life, it's easy to learn the rules but much harder to master them. Once you learn how to control what you think, feel, and do daily, the sky's the limit.

Here are three steps on how to deliberately attract something you want in your life.

Step One - Identify and Highlight Your Desire

The first step is to identify what you want in your life. This must be something that you really, truly desire. Think about what matches your criteria or whatever comes to mind. I'd suggest you write a list of all the things you want and then narrow them down to the top three or four interests that you have.

Remember that the key is finding what you really want in life, not something that's just a fleeting thought or something that sounds good when you first read about it. Whatever approach you take, the most important thing to remember is that you know what you want and give it as much clarity as you can.

Step Two - Give That Desire Your Attention

The second step is to give that desire your attention. This may be a little bit tricky for some people, especially if they tend to worry too much about the 'what ifs' of life. What you're going to do here is imagine yourself living with what it is that you want in your life. In other words, you're not just going to sit there musing about it.

Imagining life with that one thing is a potent technique because once your mind starts putting together the images, it's easier for your brain to accept this as a possibility, whether or not it's actually possible right now.

There are two sub-steps you need to follow here, the first being that you must feel good about it. If you don't, that's okay too because there are some other techniques to help you raise your vibration. These will help you make your visualization as powerful as possible, regardless of any negative emotions you may have. For example, if you imagine having a million dollars and you think that sounds great, but then your mind starts worrying about what will happen when the money runs out, there's nothing wrong with this. What you need to do is replace those negative emotions with positive ones.

You could say;

'A million dollars would give me so much freedom. I'd be able to go wherever I wanted whenever I wanted and have a job that really inspires me.;

The second step in this process is to feel it as if it's happening right now. If you're sitting in a chair, focus on the sensation of being in that chair. Feel the weight of your body on it, and focus on the sensation moving up through your legs.

If you're not in a chair right now, imagine yourself sitting there. Really get into this feeling, and focus on these sensations until they're so real to you that it feels like you could reach out and touch them if you wanted to.

You can do this for a few minutes, or you can do it for a whole 45-minute visualization session, depending on what works best for you.

In case this sounds difficult to understand, here's another example:

Take a deep breath right now and feel the air filling up your lungs. In case you're not sure how to do this, start by taking a deep breath in and holding it for a few seconds. Then release it and feel your lungs deflating back to their normal state. Once you've done that, do it again, taking an even deeper breath. Filling up your lungs with fresh air feels pretty good, right?

Do this over and over again, each time filling your lungs with even more fresh air than before.

You can feel your chest expanding more and more with each breath. As you continue this breathing process, narrow down your vision of what you want to achieve. Imagine you're filling your body up with your desires and the emotions you'll experience when you fulfill the goal you're focusing on. Fill your body with these feelings in the same way you're filling it with your breath.

Feel those emotions just as vividly.

Picture yourself living the life of your dreams and feel your body filling up with overwhelming excitement! If you're focusing on something specific, try to make this image as clear as possible.

For example, if you imagine a life where you're financially secure. Imagine checking your bank statement and seeing $50,000 in your account. Really feel how secure that will make you feel. How safe. How hard you've worked and how rewarding it will be to have that amount of money. The more emphasis you can put on these emotions, the more powerful the manifestation will be.

Remember to keep taking deep breaths while you do this. Keep going until the excitement explodes inside of you, making it impossible for you to contain it any longer!

On a final note, it's important to remain aware of any negative thoughts that pop up during this process. If you're envisioning the money in your bank account, but a thought pops in that goes, 'Well, that's never going to happen, imagine how much hard work that would be,' note it down.

Do not get carried away by the thought, instead acknowledge its existence and then try to reverse engineer it. Think about why you had that thought and where that thought originated from in your life. You may need to work on healing that part of your life to prevent it from holding you back.

Step Three - Allow it to Happen

The last step in this process is to allow whatever you want to manifest. It sounds simple, and the concept is simple, but it can take some time to put into practice. It will require a little bit of faith, but it's achievable with the kind of mindset we've been nurturing throughout this book.

Allow yourself to believe that what you're manifesting is already yours. Every time you think about it, believe that it's going to come true. You have to truly believe that your desire is possible. The Law of Attraction will pick it up and take over when you do this.

The trick is to maintain those feelings of excitement and happiness that you felt when you first identified what it was that you wanted. Make it a habit to think this way, and whenever you experience negative thoughts, identify them and figure them out.

Your mind is very good at spotting whether or not you're genuinely excited about something, even more so than it can determine if something is actually possible or not.

Just let go and let nature take its course, but never take your eyes off the prize. This may sound a little contradictory to what I said earlier about focusing on the journey, but it's like driving a car.

You get in your car and head towards your destination. You may take a couple of twists and turns, maybe a diversion here or there, you may listen to some new songs on the radio, and you may even stop for a while somewhere along the way, but having a destination will give you the direction and the motivation to keep moving forward, and eventually, you'll get there.

The Law of Attraction will be very grateful for your help in this journey, and you'll find that it'll pick up the pace when you're not pulling against it, giving you even more reasons to feel excited about what's happening right now, so stop being so hard on yourself.

The Power of Visualization

The process you've just gone through is a simple way to tap into the power of visualization. You've visualized what you want to manifest, focusing on more than just imagining it as a passing thought. You've spent a lot of energy visualizing what you want, and this affirming process will help you manifest what you want.

If you want to make the most of the Law of Attraction and truly want to manifest the life you want, learning and mastering visualization techniques will be one of the most powerful steps you can take.

In a nutshell, visualization is the practice of repeating images in your mind to help you achieve something specific. It's about seeing what you want to have a clearer image of what it is you're striving for. You can do this in your mind's eye by creating vision boards, through art, or other visual techniques, instead of just thinking about your desire.

We all do this to some degree or another. You have, or have had, dreams and goals that have driven you forward. For example, when we think about getting a job we want after school, we imagine having the role and what people will say when they see how great we look in our uniform (or suit, etc.).

When you speak in public, whether you're pitching an idea to your boss or a new client, giving a speech at a wedding, or graduating college, you may visualize what it would be like to stand up on the stage, give it your all, and to see everyone cheering, clapping, and shouting your name. That's visualization.

This is very similar to the practice of meditation in many regards, but is often used to create the future that you want. To visualize something so intensely that it becomes very real in your mind, manifesting what you want.

It's worth noting that this doesn't mean that just thinking about great, happy, and beautiful things will bring them into your life. The art of visualization means actually *experiencing* the emotions that come with having what you want. It's about creating the entire experience - physically, conceptually, and emotionally - in your mind so that you'll believe it yourself and see the opportunities you'll need to take to achieve it.

Your thoughts and feelings shape how your brain works, and what neural connections are made between your nerve cells. If you're constantly thinking about how much you want something, you create new neural pathways in your brain that will help you to achieve it.

This is why the people who visualize and feel like they already have what they want have a clearer vision of their future, and when the path changes (because there will always be obstacles), they can easily adapt.

This is why you must get into the habit of visualizing what you want rather than simply thinking about it; by actually putting effort into seeing something in your mind, you're creating that future for yourself. On a neurological level, the process of visualization is changing your brain to help you create what you want.

This is backed by science. A study carried out in the Cleveland Clinic Foundation in 2004 (Ranganathan et al., 2004) compared groups of weightlifters and their abilities to improve their physical finger abduction strength. There were two control groups - those who physically worked out, as in a gym or training studio, and those who worked out mentally.

The second control group would visualize every aspect of their training session in their heads, including what they did, how they felt, how their body felt, what the sounds were, and so on. They gave their visualizations as much detail as possible.

The results (after four weeks) showed that the physical workout group was able to improve their strength by 53%, whereas the visualization group improved their strength by up to 35%. That's huge, considering they weren't performing any physical workouts.

Applying this to your own life, try to understand what it's like to take action and follow through with your decisions (choosing to workout), and take the time to visualize what you want and what your goals and dreams are in as much detail as possible. You're going to drastically move towards making your dreams and goals your reality.

I know I keep saying this, but it's important to realize that visualization doesn't mean just thinking about something happening; it means actually *experiencing* it in your mind. Emotions, feelings, sounds, and all.

The more you can visualize, the more clearly you see the opportunities to help you get there. The more real these images become, the easier it is to recognize them when they become real.

This ultimately becomes a cycle that you can use to manifest anything. The stronger your belief becomes, the more vivid your images become, and the more likely that they will actually happen.

However, visualization isn't just helpful in creating opportunities; it's also helpful in dealing with problems when they arise. For example, if you visualize how to solve a problem or how to deal with an obstacle before it arises, your mind will be prepared when the time comes. If you're dealing with a difficult situation, you can spend time visualizing what solutions you could take.

If you can't come up with anything, visualize what you think your life will be like once you've overcome the problem. When you really start to feel it, you can reverse engineer how to get there. Of course, the law of attraction will continue to work in your favor and will open doors for you along the way to help you get there. That's the power of the universe at play.

Long story short, if you take the time to practice visualizing potential solutions to the different problems you're experiencing, the better you'll get at solving them when they crop up. If you're facing any kind of obstacle in life, visualization can give you the energy to tackle it head-on.

Jim Carrey is a prime example of how successful deep visualization can be.

When Jim Carrey first moved to Hollywood in 1985 with the dream of pursuing a career as an actor, he wrote himself a check for $10 million and dated it ten years in the future. Not ten years later, almost to the day in November 1995, he was hired for one of the lead roles in the hit comedy movie, Dumb and Dumber, with a contract worth, you've guessed it, $10 million.

Jim writing a check to himself was such a powerful way to visualize a goal - a constant reminder of what he's doing and what his aims were at the time. He wrote a check, creating energy sent out into the universe. This energy came back in the form of a $10 million contract, exactly when it was supposed to.

It's easy to forget that your thoughts are just as important as your actions, and I believe they're even more powerful because nothing can happen without them. The Law of Attraction is always working whether you believe it or not, so why not embrace it?

How to Avoid Non-Deliberate Attraction

I've spoken about this already, but the Law of Attraction is always working through the energy you put out into the universe, regardless of whether you're intentionally putting it out or not. While the techniques above are about deliberately manifesting, this second half is all about minimizing the chances of non-deliberate attraction of something you don't want.

The Law of Attraction allows you to have your desires, but it doesn't mean that they will automatically come into being. You've got to be careful about the kind of energy you're putting out because if your focus is on something in your life that you don't want, it's impossible for the Law of Attraction to get rid of it because your attention is on it.

Here's an example.

Let's say you want to lose weight, but there's a tub of ice cream in the fridge. Every time you open the fridge, you're going to see that tub of ice cream, and because it's on your mind and within your environment, you're going to want to eat it. Now, this poses a lot of issues.

You can sit and visualize a healthier weight vividly, and this will put the matching vibrational energy out into the universe. However, every time you open your fridge, you'll get thoughts that affirm your desire to eat the ice cream. The longer it sits there, the higher this vibration will be, and you'll cave eventually, manifesting the life where you eat ice cream.

Because you ate the ice cream, which went against your goal, you now think of yourself as someone who sets goals and can't stick with them. The next time you set a goal, you'll have the thought that you're someone who fails, and if you continue doubting yourself, this is the life you'll manifest, thus you'll be someone who fails whatever goal you set.

This is a dangerous spiral, and the longer it goes on, the more 'in the rut' you'll be, making it even harder to turn things around. Of course, there is a way to pull yourself out of this rut.

There are going to be victories along the way. You might ace a test, get into a new relationship you're really happy with, or get a promotion at work - all positive things that are going to raise your vibrations. You'll ebb and flow throughout your life, but if you can become increasingly conscious and aware of it, you'll massively reduce the risk of going the way you don't want to go.

So the best thing to do when you decide to lose weight? Go all in and chuck the ice cream. Commit and affirm that you're someone who eats healthy. This is how attention works. In *Atomic Habits*, the best-selling book on forming new habits written by James Clear, he mentions one of the best ways to form new habits is to put the thing you want to focus on in plain view so you're constantly focusing on it, drawing your attention to it.

For example, if you want to create the habit of playing the guitar or manifest your life as a guitarist, put your guitar in plain sight, so you're always seeing it. The more you see it, the more you visualize yourself playing it, and you'll start to send your life in the direction you want it to go.

It takes immense willpower and self-discipline to resist something that's right in front of you, especially in favor of some invisible, intangible thing. You might be able to do it once or twice, but it's not a sustainable approach, and you will cave at some point.

This is what I mean by non-deliberate attraction. You may spend time visualizing a healthy lifestyle, genuinely thinking about how it would feel to be your future self in a lifestyle you're happy with, feeling those emotions, and doing everything you can to manifest your dreams, and it might work.

For the first few days or the week, you might be doing really well and finding it works so well, but as soon as you see that ice cream and your attention switches, so does your energy, so does your vibrational frequency, and thus you go back to where you started. You've just non-deliberately attracted the thing you didn't want by emitting that energy.

So, what does this mean for you?

Well, if you want to truly manifest what you want and avoid attracting what you don't want, you need to take steps to remove those things you don't want. This means getting rid of the ice cream and basically minimizing what you don't want to manifest. If you're trying to cut down on your phone screen time, you need to put your phone out of sight.

Of course, I'm not saying you should clear out everything in your life and only have the bare essentials. You'll have things that have sentimental value and things you enjoy. You might like playing video games, and even though you think you currently play them too much, you know that you genuinely still enjoy them, so you don't want to get rid of your console entirely. That's fine.

Instead, you need to remove the things you don't want, the little reminders that keep you sending out the energy you don't want, and replace them with reminders of the things you do want to manifest. Visual reminders like this are so powerful, even if it's something as small as a Post-It note on your front door saying, 'I am going to have a good day today.'

It's a process of minimizing your life and then hyper-focusing on what you want.

Like your thoughts, you must reduce and get rid of anything that stimulates negative energy within you and your life. Pay attention to your thoughts as you go through your life. I had a friend who was incredibly into the game League of Legends, and you could very easily say he was addicted to it. He spent hours on it every day, religiously, for more than three years.

When he decided it was ruining his life and his mental health and it was time to get off it, he worked really hard for so long, and even sought therapy to overcome his addiction. A year or so later, he had finally managed to give it up. However, he still really loved League of Legends.

He loved the characters, the artwork, the style, and especially the music, and when the studios started releasing music albums, he couldn't help but listen to them. However, with such visual and audible connection to the game, he couldn't help but pick it up again.

After everything he had been through, he went back to the game because he'd put himself in a position to attract that energy, putting him back at square one. He had to start the process all over again.

I'm sure you've been in the same position. Where you've given up a bad habit or replaced it with a better, more beneficial one when something happens and you relapse, ending up back where you were. This is all because of non-deliberate attraction.

Whether it's with your thoughts, emotions, feelings, or something in your physical environment, if you keep having these negative thoughts, you're asking the universe for something bad instead of something good.

Here's another example. Let's say you wake up feeling

awful. You end up arguing with your partner and storm out of the house to go to work. Now, in this lapse of self-control, you've just sent out a ton of negative energy, and while you may not want this, the Law of Attraction won't stop it from happening.

It's the energy you've put out, so it's the energy you'll get back. This is why people have bad days and will rarely just have a single bad experience or a bad moment. One thing happens, the person gets annoyed, sad, or stressed, and it continues to happen repeatedly.

You might miss your train, trip, spill tea down your new shirt, forget everything you needed for an upcoming meeting, and so on. In more intense situations, perhaps if you've been cheating people, hurting people, or otherwise causing harm, you may find you lose your relationship, lose your job, get arrested, or experience other kinds of other intense, life-changing negative circumstances all at once. This is the build-up of negative energy coming back to you.

You're not going to be able to stay in control all the time. Sometimes, you just need to go through a bad time to learn something, but even during the more challenging days, you should still be able to take note of how you're feeling, allowing you to choose how you want to act and therefore what energy you're sending out into the universe.

Using this same example, if you're in a rotten mood and your partner is winding you up, you might feel all this negative energy building up, but instead of releasing it to your partner, you choose to say that you're in a bad mood and not in the right headspace to deal with the situation, but you will give it your attention later.

You can then go through your day venting out the negative energy in a healthy way, thus managing your decisions and actions and turning potentially negative energy into mindful positive energy, which the Law of Attraction will respond to accordingly, mostly in your favor.

How to Bring Deliberate Attraction into Your Life

So, with all this in mind, how can you start deliberately attracting what you want into your life? Let's get actionable with everything we've learned so far. Here are the steps you need to know!

1. Stop what you're doing and become mindful

This will take a bit of practice, but this is the best place to start, not just for this step but for your entire journey into tapping into the power of the Law of Attraction. Your mind is always working, and you're always putting energy out into the world, so start by understanding what energy that is.

Whenever your mind starts wandering, bring yourself back to the current moment and focus on your five senses: sight, smell, touch, taste, and sound.

If you can't get away from where you are (you may be at work or in a public space), focus on how your body feels. If you're comfortable, if there's a breeze, or you can feel the sun on your skin, take a mental note of it.

Right now, let's say you're sitting in a chair. As you read this, feel the sensation of your body weighing down into the chair. Feel that point of contact between you and the object. Turn your focus to this book or your Kindle in your hand. Feel that sensation of contact. Take a moment to look away from this writing and really feel it.

If you want to enhance the experience, take three long deep breaths. Be in control. Deeply inhale through your nose, fill up your lungs and feel your chest expand, your shoulders rising. Inhale for four seconds and hold for six seconds, as long as you can remain comfortable.

Now slowly exhale through your mouth and feel your body deflate, chest dropping, and shoulders lowering. Exhale for seven seconds. Repeat three times, and as you do so, keep your focus on the sensation of contact. Now, notice how quiet your mind gets while you do this.

As you improve your ability to focus, you'll be able to sit in this state of peace, even for only a few seconds, before the thoughts start coming back. Notice these thoughts. It really helps to do this with a piece of paper and a pen nearby so you can write down your thoughts.

Be clear, and write down anything that comes to mind. This is how you'll be able to find clarity with the thoughts and energy you're putting out.

2. Know what you want from life and be clear with it

Not everyone knows exactly what they want or, more importantly, why they want something, so take some time to sit and think about what you want. What's important to you? What do you want in your life? Do you want a relationship, friendship, great health, or money? It really doesn't matter what you want, it's the fact that you want it.

For each thing you find yourself thinking about, write it down in order of importance. Of course, it's okay if this means brainstorming and prioritizing them later.

Once you've picked out what you want, focus on the top one to three items on your list and zero in on what this goal means for you.

This is where the power of visualization comes into play, and you don't just have to do it in your head. Try to focus on what works for you. You might journal daily and jot down all your ideas and thoughts. You could do this by writing prompts like;

- I am powerful

- I live a healthy lifestyle

- I am responsible with my money

- I deserve meaningful and fulfilling relationships

- I am grateful for being me

- I exercise regularly

- I am someone who is practicing a daily yoga routine.

Or whatever it is you want to focus on. You could write these down on Post-It notes and put them around you. You could speak these affirmations or describe your perfect lifestyle in the mirror every morning. You could write a short story in a Word document where you're the main character, and you write, in detail, what a day in your new life would be like.

It's all about trying new techniques and seeing what you enjoy and what works best for you.

For me, I loved to act it out. Trying to improve my mental health, I started taking daily walks a few years ago where I would walk around the block for half an hour, getting my body moving and making sure I was getting some fresh air.

During these walks, I would think about owning a business, my relationships with people, and my dream of writing books. I would literally act out writing at a desk. I would act out reading passages of my book to a crowd in a bookstore as part of the launch promo. I would imagine signing books for a fan.

This was an impactful way for me to visualize what I

wanted in life, getting so excited about what was to come and what I could do. It became all I thought about. I set the ball in motion, sending that energy out into the universe, and a few years later, here we are, my book out into the world.

I manifested it and made it happen, and you can too!

3. Use positive language when defining what you want

Now that you have a clear idea of what you want, it's time to focus on the details. It's all well and good visualizing what you want and saying positive affirmations, but you need to focus on the language to ensure that you're actually attracting the right energy.

To start attracting your desires, you need to think about what you want in positive ways. The more specific your requests are, the better. Instead of saying, 'I want to be happy,' say, 'I am so happy now that I have this.'

The more confident you are when writing down your goals, the easier they will come to fruition.

If you're aiming for something small, such as a new car, write, 'I am so happy and grateful now that I have this shiny new car!' If you want to attract more money into your life, be confident and include words of confidence such as 'I am so happy and grateful now that money pours easily and abundantly into my life!'

Remember that the universe will deliver what you ask for, not necessarily what you want. So make sure your words reflect your true desires and not what you think will happen. If your desires won't create any more pain than they will pleasure, it's a good idea to be as specific as possible with your wording. Are you trying to attract love into your life? Be careful with how you phrase it. 'I am so happy to have the most amazing, loving relationship in my life now!' is better than saying, 'I want a boyfriend/girlfriend now! The former leaves no room for error, whereas the latter can cause great disappointment, for example, if you enter a toxic relationship or one that just isn't meant to be.

Define your desires as precisely as possible, and then work on using each sentence to put more and more positive energy onto the results you want. Keep telling yourself that things will get better until they do; speak more about how beautiful things are once you have them than the pain and struggle of not having them. Once you start noticing a difference, keep practicing until you find your voice and then let it shine without hesitation or negativity.

4. Be ready for your desires to come true

To get what you want, you need to be willing to receive it. If there's anything that you're holding on to that will prevent your desire from coming true, let go of it now. For example, if you've just given up smoking and are feeling really proud of yourself but hold on to the idea that you never quit for long, then you won't be ready to receive the desire to quit smoking (you're not open to change).

In this example, if you leave your pack of cigarettes in a drawer 'in case you need them later,' it's clear you're not ready to give up smoking; thus, the Law of Attraction ensures that you won't. Regardless of what your desire is, it's important to stack the odds in your favor. This means clearing out the things that will hold you back and bringing more things into your life that will maximize the kind of energy you want to send out.

5. Create a ritual for attracting your desires into your life

You might decide that every morning when you wake up, you will write down five things that you are grateful for before writing down your goals. Maybe every time you walk through a door, you will declare that your desired outcome is already met and give thanks for it being so.

In my own life, when I was in the process of manifesting a healthy lifestyle, I would always reward myself for running during the week. This could be a movie night with a friend, a trip out, or even a nice snack (I'm a sucker for chips and hummus). It was my ritual, and so I manifested my life. I became healthier, happier, and more fulfilled with how I was spending my time.

The more you open yourself up to deliberate attraction, what you want will make its way to you. This is the power of habit. You need to embed your affirmations as part of your everyday routine, so it becomes second nature. The easiest way to do this is to define what it is you're going to do and then set it in motion.

Pick the action, the time, and the place you're going to do it, and then practice. Set up reminders to help maximize your chances of doing it. Remember, if you're practicing your affirmation, say, in front of your mirror every morning while you're brushing your teeth, then taking action like putting a Post-It note on your mirror to remind you to repeat the affirmation will help you attract the kind of energy you're looking for.

6. Let go of your attachment to how it's going to come about

When we focus on our desires and allow them to manifest, we become attached (in a good way) to the outcome matching what we envisioned. Sometimes though, we can get so attached to how we see it playing out that we miss what is happening right in front of us.

For example, you might think that your partner will propose when the time is exactly right and not a minute before or after, but this often leaves you feeling frustrated as everything else seems to be coming into place except what you want. This is only going to amplify the negative vibrations you're living with.

The point to remember here is to let go of the attachment and your expectations, and instead focus on what you're trying to manifest and how you're going to make it happen. As long as you keep putting those positive vibrations out, the Law of Attraction will make it happen. However, some laws need to be met.

For example, you could manifest a million dollars, but it's not going to happen instantly in most cases. You won't wake up and find a million dollars in your bank account or under your bed. There may be other areas in your life you need to work on before you're ready for your manifestation, such as your job or the way you use money as an escape from your day-to-day life. If you were given a million dollars, you might spend it all on things that don't matter, and it would have been a waste. Because there's no balance, you're not ready.

You need to go through the process of learning how to manage your money, acquiring the skills you need, and being at the right point in your life where the Law of Attraction will manifest the million dollars you've asked for. Remember how Jim Carrey had to wait ten years for his manifestation to happen? The same applies to you.

In the meantime, keep focusing on your end goal, keep visualizing it, and keep aiming to make it happen. Let go of the expectation of how and when it will manifest, and just focus on the fact that it will as long as you keep heading in the right direction.

7. Don't go looking for reasons why it won't work or give up when you find them

This often stops people from using the Law of Attraction effectively. Your mind will tell you that this won't work or that it isn't possible for you. Don't let it talk you out of what you want.

You need to be mindful of your thoughts. I have to repeat this because it's so important, and if you're not aware that it can happen, it will happen without you realizing.

So, say you're manifesting a million dollars, and it doesn't come after a week, and you think to yourself, 'Oh wow, that was so unrealistic to ask for a million dollars. Like that will ever happen.' You've just put that energy out into the universe, and so you give up. Guess what, that's your vibration, and now you won't manifest it.

Throughout your life, you're going to see signs that may suggest for you not to go for what you're aiming for. For example, other opportunities for other jobs or other relationships may come your way that could take you down a completely different path. This is because there are multiple ways to reach your path, the result of which will depend on your manifestations and your choices.

For example, let's say you want to be successful in your career. You could be successful in the job you're currently in via a promotion, by getting a job in a new company, or by starting your own business. When you're manifesting career success, you'll manifest these opportunities at different times, but you need to esnure you remain headstrong with your ventures.

Remember, you should have a clear idea of what you want and what you're trying to achieve. You should see it clearly from the beginning, and it's important to recognise that other opportunities can been seen as temptations or even tests.

Treating them as tests from the universe gives you a chance to check in with whether or not you actually want what you think you want. If you're able to stay on track and pursue what you want, then it shows you're committed, therefore sending out certain vibrations to the universe that you want what you want, thus you'll be capable of manifesting it.

For me, when I told my parents I was going to start writing books, they would say things like 'Isn't that really difficult to get into?' and 'I don't know how you'll be able to support yourself.'

These are vibrations that I could have allowed to stop me from heading down my path, but I chose to let those anxieties go and instead work on affirming myself and, well, you're reading the result!

If you're serious about what you're aiming for, these are signs that should be ignored.

If you do encounter resistance on your journey, it's important to acknowledge it but divert your focus away from them and refocus your thoughts on what you want. This will increase the amount of focus you have on what you want, therefore sending out more powerful energy to the universe, and you'll receive even more powerful energy.

In summary, if you combine all these tactics, you'll allow deliberate attraction to start working for you, and you will notice your dreams beginning to manifest into reality. You will have taken control of the Law of Attraction, and it will provide for you. You'll be able to use the Law of Attraction more efficiently, and that means even greater things for your life.

Of course, it takes time and practice. You're going to ebb and flow through the path significantly since the world around you is constantly changing, but that's all part of the journey. The Law of Attraction is the source of power that allows you to live the life you want.

Skills to Practice to Better Deliberate Attraction

If you want to get better at practicing deliberate attraction, there are some skills you can work on to develop your ability to manifest the life you want. These will be some quick-fire tips that can help you move along and perfect your skills as you go and help you manifest even better results.

1. Focus on having fun

Pursuing your desires should be an enjoyable experience, so if you're not enjoying yourself, then this isn't deliberate attraction, no matter what it looks like to everyone around you. If your life is full of stress and frustration, this energy will manifest in the form of problems that prevent you from getting what you want when you want it.

2. Focus on what you do have instead of what you don't

When we focus on what we do have, we give thanks for

this abundance, allowing the energy to flow more freely.

3. Be patient, persistent, and positive

It can take time for what you want to come about, but if you're patient and persistent, then one day, the Law of Attraction will work quickly enough for you to see results in your life. Whatever else happens, stay positive because this energy will be present in your thoughts and emotions, and it could even affect the people around you.

4. Focus on true feelings

For example, if you're going for a promotion at work or looking to find a partner, focus on how you would feel getting into that position and what life would be like when you have it or have achieved it. Of course, I'm not saying you should dismiss how you feel now and always live with your head in the future, but when it comes to visualizing and the process of manifesting, focusing on the feelings rather than the thing itself is what makes a difference.

5. Focus on having fun and appreciate what you have, not on the outcome

We become unhappy when we focus only on an outcome without considering how much fun it is and how grateful we are for everything we already have. This is because it is easy to pressure ourselves and others around us if we feel like things aren't happening quickly enough.

6. Stay in the present moment more often

You can use past experiences of having fun or being positive as a way to draw in positive feelings when you're manifesting something new. However, you need to stay in the present moment more often than not because dwelling on past experiences can lead us into unhelpful patterns of thought that prevent us from seeing the good that's already there or appreciating what we have right now.

7. Allow things to unfold naturally

It can be tempting to try and force things to happen too quickly, but that will block the law of attraction from working because it isn't going to align with what you want. If you let things unfold naturally, the universe will do everything for you, so all you have to do is sit back and allow your desires to manifest.

8. Let go of the outcome

I know that this might sound a little contradictory because it goes against everything I've been saying about focusing on what you want, but there's also a time to let go and welcome whatever comes about.

For example, if you're looking for a new job, you should welcome all possibilities because you don't know what will happen. You might lose your job only to end up in a new job which is where you'll find your manifested satisfaction, or you might end up going down a new path, such as starting your own business, which you might have never considered.

It's all about affirming your desires for your career and then trusting that the law of attraction has your back.

If you can focus on bringing these skills into your life, you'll find it much easier to manifest what you desire, and the results will be much more powerful.

Try not to be overwhelmed by these principles, and instead of focusing on all of them, take time to figure out which ones work for you.

These eight techniques will give you a much-needed foundation if you're starting out with the Law of Attraction or when you are in doubt about how it works.

CHAPTER SIX

How Thoughts and Words
Can Lead Your Journey

*"Never underestimate the power of thought; it
is the greatest path to discovery."*
— Idowu Koyenikan

There's no denying that the words you think, say, and
write are important factors to consider when it comes
to the Law of Attraction. The Law of Attraction and
words are inextricably linked. Saying words out loud,
chanting them to yourself or someone else, or writing

messages are all ways of communicating with the universe.

And when you're communicating with the universe, you're putting the Law of Attraction into practice. So, this begs the question, how can you master the art of using words to bring yourself a step closer to mastering the Law of Attraction?

Words You Speak and Think

Your words are immensely powerful. If you are constantly bombarding your mind with negative thoughts or putting yourself down, you'll only feel worse about yourself and attract more negativity into your life.

This is because when you say things out loud, it triggers the same emotion in the person saying it and anyone listening. This means that if you're speaking negatively about yourself, people will instantly pick up on it and feel the same way you do.

Your words also become habitual; the more often you speak a specific phrase or word, the more natural it becomes to you and others around you. The best way to master your words is to choose them carefully.

The words you speak are just as powerful as the thoughts you think. If the thoughts are negative, they could have a more profound impact on your life than you realize. For instance, if someone is constantly thinking about being alone or never finding love, they may find that their life starts to reflect this.

On the other hand, if a person is constantly speaking words of love and appreciation, they may find that they feel more loved or appreciated in their life. Both these examples show how your thoughts and words can impact the world around you.

Writing Out Affirmations

You've probably heard of affirmations before but haven't known exactly what to do with them. Well, that's about to change.

It can be challenging to speak affirmations rather than just thinking about them because you're afraid of coming off as cocky or self-centered. The truth is, you probably already use affirmations all the time without even realizing it. For example, when someone says, 'you look great today,' you're likely to respond with a 'thank you' rather than thinking about how great the other person looks.

That's an affirmation in itself, and it has a greater effect on your life if you make a conscious effort to do it instead of just letting it happen naturally. You can use this same strategy when writing out affirmations, and every time you write one, say it aloud.

This will help to strengthen the affirmation's effect on your life and how you feel because then the words are much more powerful. When writing affirmations, follow these basic rules:

Make each affirmation personal. You may already have a list of affirmations written, but when you write them out for yourself, make sure they are different every time. If you notice that you tend to repeat affirmations, switch them up or get rid of them altogether.

Be specific in your affirmations. It's very difficult to be positive about something if it doesn't apply to your own life, but if you're very specific in your affirmations, it makes it easier to believe in and more powerful. Instead of convincing yourself that you are successful with money or weight loss, write the exact amount of money you want to be earning per year or what you want your ideal weight to be.

Be realistic about your affirmations. If you've already written out some affirmations that are too unrealistic for your life right now, don't be afraid to cross them out and replace them with something more realistic. This doesn't mean that you're giving up on the original affirmation; it simply means that they're two separate things.

Boost Your Confidence With Affirmations

Many people shy away from affirmations because they feel that they're being too cocky when they repeat the same phrase over and over again. They may think it's silly or way too simple a process to actually have any effect, but this is far from the truth. These are common misconceptions about positive affirmations.

In fact, a study published in the Social Cognitive and Affective Neuroscience detailed how scientists and researchers used an MRI scanner on people who were repeating positive affirmations to themselves. The results showed that the people who repeated affirmations activated the reward centers of their brain, which relates to dopamine and serotonin.

This part of your brain is pretty much responsible for making you do things in your life. Otherwise, you'd have no drive to do anything. If you're hungry, you eat food and it feels good (the release of reward chemicals) that makes you feel happy that you ate, thus you don't die of starvation.

Interestingly, we love fast food because in the past when we lived in caves and hunted our food, large sugary, high-calorie meals were ideal because they would fill us up and keep us energized for longer than an piece of fruit would, which is why we get such a feel good rush when eating junk food.

Through affirmations, you can activate these same neural pathways, therefore using them to your advantage. If you say something like, 'I will earn that promotion,' it lights up the pathways in your brain, and since all your motivations in life are influenced by this driving force, you're far more likely to take action to fulfill that idea of whatever affirmation you're telling yourself.

It all comes down to wanting something and repeating it so much that your brain hyper-focuses on making it happen. Couple this with the Law of Attraction and you'll have the perfect storm when it comes to manifesting what you want, both on a universe and individual scale.

Make your affirmations personal and realistic to your own life and you'll be able to boost your confidence while giving yourself the focus and clarity when it comes to making powerful decisions in your day-to-day life. Affirmations help you to clearly visualize what you want and help you send out the right vibrations of what you want to attract.

Try writing out ten affirmations that are personal, specific, and realistic. Write each affirmation three times each day; once in the morning, afternoon, and before bed. Bonus points for saying them out loud every time!

The Words You Speak to Others

Just like the words you speak to yourself can make a huge difference to the kind of energy you're bringing into your life, so can the words you use when speaking to or about other people.

For example, gossiping or spreading rumors about others lowers your vibrations in the same way posting a negative Tweet or listening to a negative news source does. Words are like magic, and whenever you use them, ensure you're sending the message you want to send, and you're being as concise and as specific as you can be.

You need to be aware of the words you choose when talking about other people. It's normal to let something someone has done bother you and affect your opinion of them, but that doesn't help either one of you. If you're constantly telling yourself that someone is a bad person, you're going to have a hard time believing that they could be anything else.

When speaking about other people, the words you use can either build them up or tear them down.

The Words You Speak to the Universe

The words you speak to the Universe matter. This is what affirmations are, so you want to make sure that you're saying things with the best of intentions.

The words you use when speaking to the Universe should make your life better. If there's something about your life that you don't like or wish were different, speak directly to it and tell it how you feel and what you want to happen.

Instead of telling the Universe that things will go your way or that you'll get something if it's meant to be yours, try saying, 'I accept this situation gracefully' or "I choose happiness even through any difficult times.'

Your Words Create Your Reality

Your words are your reality, your reality is what you attract. Be clear about what you want and how you'd like to see yourself. If you say 'I am beautiful' but don't believe it or act like it, the Universe will bring you more people who tell you otherwise.

However, if your words are filled with good intentions and are universal, they'll help you grow. Once you start becoming more confident with who you are and what you can do, the Universe will mirror that back to you by bringing in confident, positive beings.

And if that doesn't happen, you need to choose whether or not you want to change your words so that they can become your reality.

CHAPTER SEVEN

The Three Steps of the Law of Attraction

See yourself living in abundance and you will attract it. It always works, it works every time, with every person
- Bob Proctor

Let's focus on some practical ways of using the Law of Attraction.

You will apply this step on both a macro and micro level. You'll be able to create very big and important things by thinking about them in a very small way.

Step I: Identify Your Desire

The first step is identifying your desire. This entails stating what you want, why you want it, and how you'll know when you have it. Sometimes this is very simple, but other times it can be a little difficult to figure out exactly what we want and why we want it.

So take some time to clarify what you want. You can write down your desires or just record an audio or video, making sure to state why you want it. This helps because sometimes we have grand dreams, but they don't actually serve us in the present moment. When thinking about your desire and writing it down, you need to specify how you'll know that it has manifested. What will make this real for you?

This is important because if there's no way of measuring the outcome, it'll be hard to tell whether or not what we're looking for actually exists. It takes a lot of guesswork, which is why it's important to take the time to figure out such details.

Step Two: Belief

The second step involves figuring out how you can truly

believe that you can manifest your dream into reality. It's essential to believe fully in what you're doing to see it through to the end.

There are different ways to do this, but the best one usually comes from looking at all angles involved in what you desire. Look for others who have manifested something similar or start by manifesting something seemingly small. This could be manifesting something both positive and negative. Once you have your proof, it will be far easier for you to believe in much larger manifestations in your life.

I recently spoke with a friend who streams video games in his free time. He was playing a game and became incredibly angry and ended up being really offensive to his team players. Through these actions and words, he pushed a ton of negative vibrations out into the universe.

The next day, someone he was close to left the community for personal reasons out of the blue. Other people argued in the community text channels over something, which made the community very divisive. This all stemmed from him amplifying negative energy mindlessly in his games.

As soon as he took a moment to tone everything back

and acknowledged that his actions were wrong, he adopted a red panda with his community money and gave it to a conservation project. Everybody made up fairly quickly after this. This is how quickly the Law of Attraction can work.

Practice your visualization techniques and keep feeling the emotions and feelings you imagine you would feel if you had already achieved and accomplished that goal. This helps because it's almost like priming the subconscious mind to think that this has already happened. You can also picture how your friends and family will react when they find out about your success.

But remember, don't just be happy for yourself - take some time to revel in their joy as well! You may also want to set an ideal timeframe for your manifestation to occur so the universe knows you're being serious about what you want.

Step Three: Succeed

This final step is all about manifestation. You've set up what you want, and you have full belief that it's going to happen, but now you need to get specific with it. This means applying the techniques we've covered in this book.

Now, you'll want to create a series of commands that act as a blueprint for what you want to achieve. These should be very strong and direct statements that set a clear timeframe and lift your spirits by reminding yourself how awesome it feels to have this desire fulfilled.

Here is an example 'I am so grateful for my new car which I will receive within the next six months! And even though I am going to have a car that makes me feel happy and fulfilled, I'm going to bask in the happiness of all my friends and family as they marvel at what a wonderful person I've become.'

Keep repeating these statements and keep committing to your success. Repetition is key.

So these are the three steps to help you begin manifesting your desires into reality. Remember, it'll take some time and effort on your part, but once you see how this works, you'll want to put it into practice all the time!

CHAPTER EIGHT

Methods of Practice

This chapter is all about building on the practices in the previous chapter. If the three-step technique is the foundation, these are the intermediate and advanced steps that will help elevate what you're capable of attracting and manifesting.

The Stacking Method

This neat technique involves stacking small, medium,

and large manifestations on top of each other. It's sort of like getting the ball rolling and allowing your desires to start coming together without too much effort on your part.

So let's say you want $100 right now. That would be considered a small manifestation, so we can leave it out of the equation. But you also want a new job so you can pay your bills and have enough money to live comfortably without needing extra work. This would be considered a medium manifestation, so we'd put that in the middle column.

However, if you wanted $20,000 in your savings account, this would be considered a large manifestation that we'd put at the end.

Now we start stacking! Let's say you want $100. You'll start with the smaller manifestations first.

So $100 is a relatively small manifestation. You could get this by working a one-off job opportunity that you manifest or on your monthly pay packet. You would need to manifest this ten times, basically stacking ten manifestations on top of each other to then have $1000.

$1,000 to most people is a medium manifestation. You would then need to stack this medium manifest twenty times to get to the $20,000, which is a large manifestation. Or manifestation the small $100 manifest 200 times.

Instead of just going for a larger manifestation off the bat, it can really help to break things down and tackle them one step at a time, eventually leading to that larger manifestation.

The trick to how this works is that you'll achieve a small manifestation, and you'll get the feeling of what it feels like to successfully manifest something, which makes it far easier for you to visualize what you want because you've already experienced those feelings. Just focus on them and keep going. Repeat and repeat and repeat until your dreams come true!

The Time-Lapse Method

The Time-Lapse Technique is ideal for when you want to manifest something relatively quickly.

For example, let's say you have an urgent deadline coming up in the next week. You can use this method to speed things along by stacking small, medium, and large time lapses on top of each other, but first, here's a little explanation.

The time-lapse method literally focuses on time, and by that, I'm referring to the past, the present, and the future. What you're doing is using time in a way to help you certainly manifest your desired reality.

To do this, you need to think of an equal number of things, in this case, I'm going to choose six, since meeting a deadline is a relatively small manifestation in comparison to something like one million dollars, but it could be large for you. It depends on your perspective. Ideally, you'll want to use six things for a small manifestation, 9 to 12 for a medium one, and 15 for a large one.

Either way, it needs to be divisible by three.

What you're doing next is taking things from the past and the present. I'm thinking of six things, two from the past, two from the present, and then two from the future. I'm thinking of things that I'm grateful for and am certain of in both the past and the present and then applying them to the future, or in other words, the reality I'm manifesting.

So, using the example of meeting a deadline, my process may look a little something like this;

The Past

- I have been in this job for three years and I am capable of doing it

- I have challenged myself and met deadlines before

The Present

- I am healthy and capable to complete the work

- I have the support of my team to help me get the work done

The Future

- I will complete the work on time for the deadline

- I will complete it to the desired quality

Of course, the more points you put into your lists, the more powerful your manifestations will be. The point you need to remember is that you need to have clarity and certainty based on the past and present and you can apply these feelings to your desired future. What you list is up to you. It can be a feeling, an event, a physical object, a person, or a place. It's about figuring out what works for you.

Now, you want to bring in the power of visualizations and manifestation into this method for it to work. So go through your statements, and write them as affirmations that you're then going to stack on top of one another. For example;

- I'm grateful for my work experience and how capable I am because of it

- I'm grateful for my hard work and ability to meet deadlines

- I'm grateful I'm in a positive physical and mentally sound place

- I'm grateful for the support of my team

- I'm grateful for my commitment to my world and drive to meet my deadline

- I'm grateful for my ability to complete my work to a high quality

Through the process of stacking in this way, you'll have

the direction and focus you need to get stuff done and to manifest a successful end to your deadline.

It's not an exact science, but it can help to speed things along when you're pushed up against a deadline.

We've talked about the Law of Attraction as a way to manifest your desires or attract something you want into your life. But what if it's not always about having something tangible?

Maybe someone is sick, and you want to help them feel better. How can we use this same technique if our desires aren't always something we can see and touch?

The answer is through the art of feeling.

Let's go back to the previous example where you wanted a new job so you could pay your bills and have enough money to live comfortably without needing extra work on the side. What would it feel like if you were currently living that life?

If you're not quite sure, take some time and close your eyes. Imagine what it would be like to finally find a good job where you make enough money and no longer need to worry about paying your bills or having work on the side. You can even go as far as imagining yourself financially free and being able to spend your time doing whatever you want without having to work extra hours. Maybe you want to travel the world, start a business, or go back to school. Now, how would that feel?

There's no right or wrong answer, but if you're struggling, then I encourage you to set aside some quiet time where you can really work on answering the question.

After you've figured out what it would feel like if you had that job or enough money to pay your bills, spend some time visualizing that feeling. Imagine how good it would feel to finally be free of worry and no longer have to spend extra hours at work. If you can really put yourself in this mindset, then you're truly harnessing the power of your emotions in manifesting.

So why is it so important to be able to feel what you want? When we use our logical mind or 'head' to try and visualize or imagine something, it's only when the emotion center, also known as the heart, joins in that things start to change.

This is why, when you're trying to manifest something tangible, it's just as important to have the emotion or feeling of already having that thing for it to become real.

It's not enough just to think about paying your bills or having a new job because if you can't get yourself into the right mindset, it's not going to be possible for you to achieve these goals.

Looking at this from a different perspective helps us better understand why we can't manifest specific things. Have you ever had one of those days where you just couldn't get your mind off something? Maybe it was an ex-boyfriend or girlfriend, wanting to buy something you don't have the money for, or even just wanting to eat chocolate when you're on a diet. You know that these thoughts are making you feel bad somehow, but what good does it do us in the long run?

The answer is - absolutely nothing. All these negative thoughts produce negative emotions, and that's why it's so important to break the cycle. Meditation is one way to do this because it helps you get in touch with what your body and mind are feeling, allowing you to let go of all the things that no longer serve a positive purpose in your life, however, this is something we're going to deep dive into throughout Chapter Nine, so watch this space.

Gratitude Attraction Boosters

Gratitude is a great way to turn your feelings positive again. When you constantly focus on what you have rather than on what you don't, it helps lower stress and anxiety levels by reminding you of all the good things that are already in your life.

And this isn't just from personal experience. Anybody who talks about self-help, self-development, mindfulness, or the Law of Attraction will talk about the power of gratitude and how important it is to adopt a gratitude practice. What's more, the scientific research is very clear on the matter.

There are endless studies that show that gratitude;

- Creates better, more stable, and more fulfilling relationships

- Improves physical health

- Improves mental and psychological health

- Enhances empathy

- Lowers aggressive tendencies

- Improves quality of sleep

- Increases self-esteem and self-worth

- Improves ability to overcome and process trauma

Let's make this practical and say you're in a position where you're constantly worried about paying your bills. You could then repeat an affirmation like 'I'm grateful for all the money I have coming in and out each month and the money I already have in my account.'

You can start this affirmation as soon as you think of it, and by doing so, you immediately shift your thoughts to gratitude.

With that said, here's a list of five simple but effective affirmations for manifesting:

1) 'My desires are now manifesting quickly and easily.'

5) 'Every day and in every way, my life gets better and better.'

2) 'My work is fulfilling and enjoyable.'

6) 'I am relaxed and calm.'

3) 'I enjoy spending time with (insert name here).'

7) 'I feel successful and on track with my goals.'

8) 'I am always manifesting the right people, opportunities, and abundance in my life.'

4) 'I'm surrounded by love and light.'

9) 'I am focused, positive, and enjoying life to the fullest.'

10) 'My dreams are coming true now!'

If you can really achieve this mindset, you're genuinely harnessing the power of your emotions in manifesting.

Scripting Method for Manifesting

Another way to harness the power of your emotions is through writing. This method is also known as scripting, and it's believed to be one of the most practical manifestation techniques available. Now you might think, why would I want to write something down when I could just keep it in my head? The answer is that by writing things down, you're far more likely to follow through and take action because of the amount of energy required.

Writing out what you want allows you to visualize your goal in detail, including how it will look and feel, as well as anything else you may be feeling at the time of writing. It also serves as a reminder, so you don't forget what you set out to achieve. To sum it up, here are the steps for scripting:

1) Write what you want in present tense and use 'I am' rather than 'I want.'

2) Write down how it would feel using positive words such as happy, excited, or inspired. For example, if you want a new job, write: 'I am so happy and excited about going to work tomorrow because I have a fantastic new job.'

3) Make your list as long as you want by writing down all the things you can have or do.

4) Read your list out loud every day, a minimum of three times per day, ideally at least once in the morning before breakfast, again in the afternoon, and one more time just before you go to sleep.

5) Carry your list if possible so that you can read it throughout the day. This will allow it to sink into your subconscious and make it easier for things to manifest quickly.

6) Once you feel as though something has manifested or come to fruition, remember to stop reading your list

and take a few moments out of every day to be grateful for what you have now.

So there you go! A simple method for using the Law of Attraction that will help you feel good and become a magnet for all things positive in life.

The Manifestation Method

The manifestation method is a technique you can use to manifest something quickly. It's very similar to scripting because it involves writing down what you want, but there are a few key differences between the two methods. The first thing you need to do is write your list of goals or desires using positive words and speaking in the present tense.

You're also required to visualize what it feels like to have your goal already, but instead of doing this using positive words like excited or happy, you might find it easier actually to write down how it would feel. This can be done by thinking about the various senses and writing them all out in detail, much like a list. For instance, if you want a new job, your list might look like this:

'I am sitting in my new office, and I can smell coffee brewing in the kitchen next door; I can feel the warmth of the sun on my skin and see that it's a perfect day for working outside; I can hear people chatting away happily and the sound of the kettle boiling for tea; I can taste my lunch that's just been brought to me, and it tastes delicious.'

You might also find it helpful at this stage to imagine your goal is already achieved up until you actually receive it. So, if you want a new job, you may visualize yourself getting dressed for work, driving to the office, walking into your new office, and beginning work.

The next step is similar to scripting in that you need to read aloud what you wrote every day until you feel as though your goal has manifested or come to fruition. You should also try repeating this list of steps two more times over the course of the day.

The main difference between the two methods is that while scripting focuses on getting you to feel good and therefore attracting positivity, manifestation techniques teach you how to visualize in great detail to attract what you want. This is especially useful if something specific has been on your list of goals for a long time. The manifestation technique is so successful for this specific goal because you're able to see just how close you are to achieving it and, therefore, become even more determined than before.

So, there you have it! A simple method that uses the Law of Attraction techniques, scripting, and visualization simultaneously. Once again, manifesting something quickly using this method is all about feeling good, so make sure you feel grateful for what you already have in your life rather than focusing on how far away your goal seems.

CHAPTER NINE

Meditation and the Law of Attraction

"It is indeed a radical act of love just to sit down and be quiet for a time by yourself"
– Jon Kabat-Zinn

Many of the most successful entrepreneurs and business people in the world today attribute at least some of their success to meditation. Meditation helps to silence internal chatter and noise to focus on your goals and desires, which in turn helps you to use the Law of

Attraction more effectively.

If this is the first time you've come across the idea of meditation, relax! This chapter will explain what meditation is, why it can be so effective, and how to do it properly, and the rest of the chapter will help you create your own personalized meditation technique.

Meditation for the Law of Attraction

Meditation is an ancient practice that has been used for centuries by countless cultures to help bring peace and tranquility to the mind, body, and spirit. It's only relatively recently in human history that our busy, always-on society has become so demanding that many people find it difficult to even take a few minutes out of their day to meditate. It may seem strange that something so simple can have such a dramatic effect, but remember that there are signs that meditation has been a part of human culture since 5,000BCE, so over 7,000 years.

It's still practiced to this day, and for good reason. Meditation is very similar to the process of writing your goals down in that it allows you to clear away all of the excess information floating around in your mind to make room for what really matters. It helps you learn to focus on what you want rather than what you don't want, and this is especially important when practicing the Law of Attraction.

If meditation sounds a bit too new-age for you, think of it as simply taking some time out to relax and slow down; whether it's during your lunch break or on the bus home, even five minutes can make a huge difference.

The Power of Meditation for Attracting What You Want

Most people don't bother meditating, but those who do often see their lives change in ways they never thought possible. To many, it's a practice that brings up many conditioned thoughts, such as it being a practice used for clearing your mind of all thoughts or tidying up all of the negativity cluttering up your mind, but it's so much more than that.

You can use it as a way to become more present, allowing you to watch out for opportunities and signs from the universe. It can help you increase your levels of self-discipline, and most notably, in the context of this book, it can be utilized as a tool for harnessing the power of the Law of Attraction and manifestation.

It can also be used to help you get to know yourself better. You can calm your mind and focus on your thoughts, allowing you unique insight into how you feel and what you're thinking about. This will ensure you can see what thoughts you're having and, therefore, what vibrations you're putting out into the universe. This is a way of taking control over your deliberate and non-deliberate manifestations.

In this section, I will break down meditation and how you can use it as a powerful technique for getting close and comfortable with the Law of Attraction. Let's start with the basics and work through everything we've learned so far.

Creating Your Own Meditation Technique

There are endless ways you can go about meditating You can sit in a quiet room with your legs crossed for ten minutes in a traditional meditation pose, or you can mindfully drink a takeaway cup of coffee on a busy train. There are so many variations to meditation, but the trick is to experiment to see what works for you.

Everybody in the world is different and has different ways of thinking, so you need to be creative and open to trying new things until you can find a way of meditating that really does work for you. This is what it means to create your own meditation technique. However, try not to treat it as a mission or a chore for the best results. Instead, have fun with it and treat it as a journey.

So, where do you start?

First, start with mastering the foundations of meditation, and remember, meditation isn't just something you can learn in one day and then you're done for life. It's a process that will continuously evolve throughout your life, and you can always go deeper into your practice. But for now, let's start with the essentials, especially if you're new to the practice.

Start by finding a quiet space in a place you're comfortable and sit in silence with your eyes closed. Focus on your breathing. Slow down your breathing. Inhale through your nose for five seconds, hold for six seconds, and then exhale through your mouth slowly and steadily for eight seconds. If you can't do these times, then adjust and perform this exercise in a way that suits you.

As you repeat this cycle of inhaling and exhaling, focus on the little pauses, the gaps, and the moments of silence between your inhales and exhales. You'll notice there's a small moment of stillness as you switch. This act of focusing will help you become more aware of your thoughts and the type of thinking that is manifesting your reality.

As you sit, cycle through this breathing pattern for several minutes as you pay attention to your mind. Try to see what thoughts come to mind naturally and what kind of patterns they have. Do not get carried away with the thought itself but rather to see it from an external perspective, as though you're watching your thoughts.

Label the thoughts as positive, negative, or by their subject, and then let them go. This will take some practice, and you're going to notice over and over again that you fall into the process of thinking whatever thought comes up, and that's okay. Be compassionate with yourself and forgive yourself if you get caught up in your thinking and realize you've spent most of your session lost in thought.

This is just what happens, so be patient with yourself, and I can assure you that you'll get better with time. Meditation is a skill that can be practiced and refined. Now that you know the basics, you can start customizing it to suit you and make it work in the best way for you.

For example, do you prefer having a routine where you meditate in the morning or at night? Do you like silence or having music on in the background? Do you like guiding your own meditation, or do you prefer using guided meditation? Perhaps meditation classes work best for you? Do you prefer meditation for listening to your thoughts or visualizing your manifestations? Do you use meditation as a mixture of both?

This is what I mean by creating your own meditation routine. A routine is essential as it is an everyday practice, but how you go about doing it is entirely up to you. It will take time and experimentation, a life-long process where you'll dip and dive into various forms of practice.

As you continue to refine your meditation process, try

to develop a practice where you meditate at least once per day.

Start by setting aside five minutes each time and build on it. Try visualizing and being peaceful. Try meditating and then writing your thoughts down. If you're looking to take your Law of Attraction practice to the next level, using meditation is definitely an essential part of the process, as we'll continue to explore now.

We live in a world full of distractions, and it's almost impossible to clear away everything that constantly flows into our minds. Even when we're relaxing, we often think about work, relationships, money, and other worries; this is why most people find it difficult to relax and enjoy themselves.

Meditation helps you to lose all of your worries and find your focus, but there's another reason why it works so well when combined with the Law of Attraction; when you meditate, you are sending out a signal to the universe, which says, 'focus on me.'

Remember, this isn't about living your life without making mistakes or without ever worrying about the future; rather, it's about finding peace and harmony so that your thoughts are always positive. When you meditate, you're effectively asking the universe to help you manifest everything that you want into your life, and as a result of doing this regularly, many people experience phenomenal results.

The Benefits of Meditation

Now, you don't just have to take the words of the monks from centuries ago, nor the vouching of a Silicon Valley CEO to believe that meditation works and can bring a range of benefits into your life. Scientific research has proven it so many times. In fact, the only thing which seems to stop people from meditating regularly is their own minds.

So, what are these benefits?

- Meditation increases your levels of concentration and focus. This is ideal for manifesting and using the Law of Attraction because you need to be capable of focusing and concentrating on what you want.

- Meditation reduces stress and anxiety. Everyone has different triggers which make them stressed, and it's important to be able to deal with this before you start working with the universal Law of Attraction; otherwise, your mind will constantly be clouded by negative thoughts and feelings.

- Meditation helps you to sleep better at night. This is particularly useful for those who have a hard time sleeping, and it's all about being able to relax.

- Meditation helps you to improve your general health. As a direct result of feeling less anxious and stressed, your body will experience the positive impacts as well – including lower blood pressure and easier breathing.

- Meditation makes you feel happier. The more you meditate, the more you'll feel happy with yourself and about your life, which has a knock-on effect of making people around you much happier!

- Meditation has been proven to help with weight loss. This is because mindfulness meditation helps you become more aware of your thoughts and feelings. Therefore, you're able to notice your cravings for food or snacks and identify your triggers. Becoming more mindful can ensure you don't fall into your old habits as often.

- Meditation is said to help people live longer because it reduces the risk of illnesses associated with stress and anxiety, such as heart disease or certain types of cancer.

This list is enough to encourage many people to practice meditation daily, but there are many more benefits. How many people would have thought that meditation helps you to sleep better?

It's incredible how it can change your life and make everything better.

Life is hard and full of distractions, making maintaining focus tough. However, through meditation, you can learn to control your thoughts and feelings rather than them controlling you; this enables you to manifest the things that matter to you much more effectively because just thinking about them isn't enough.

The way you meditate can vary, and there are so many techniques, such as guided meditation or simply just closing your eyes and listening to the sounds around you. Some people prefer to wear earplugs while meditating, while others like to listen to music. The important thing is that you find a way that works for you and try your best to meditate daily.

The Five Steps of Meditation

Meditating is quite a simple process in theory, but the reality of the practice makes it more than just sitting and doing nothing. It requires mindfulness and bringing awareness to your thoughts, which can get uncomfortable from time to time.

If you're dealing with difficult emotions, such as stress, anxiety, pain, or even depression, you may try to meditate, only to find your mind thinking a million thoughts a minute. It happens. You may not want to think about any of it and would prefer to resort to your usual coping mechanism, but in times like this, meditation is essential.

When I was severely depressed and thought of taking my own life, I suppressed these thoughts until it was basically impossible to meditate because those feelings would come back up. Perhaps in your own experiences, whether through stress, anger, or sadness, you've tried meditating but find it uncomfortable to sit with these feelings.

The best way to address this (in addition to seeking professional help if you need it or getting involved in other forms of self-care) is to practice meditation regardless and do what you can.

Even if you're not 'going through something,' you may still find your mind wandering dramatically while meditating, and that's fine. You may have vivid aspirations come to mind, or you may feel plans manifesting themselves, and that's fine. Meditation is about being able to come to terms with what 'is.'

Meditation can also be used as a tool for accessing other things, such as maximizing the power of the Law of Attraction. For now, let's start with the basics.

1. Find a quiet space where you can meditate without any distractions.

2. Sit in an upright position with your feet flat on the floor and your arms resting by your side.

3. Close your eyes and focus on the spot between your eyebrows – known as the third eye chakra!

4. Breathe deeply through your nose and imagine that you're breathing in negative energy and exhaling positive energy.

If your mind begins to wander, just bring it back to the third eye chakra and focus on your breathing.

5. Continue this for as long as you need, making sure every time that your mind starts to wander to bring it back by focusing on the third eye chakra.

That's pretty much it.

It doesn't matter how long you meditate, as long as you make it a part of your daily routine and try to sit in the same place every single day. This will help to make it easier when trying to focus because after some time, your mind begins to associate that space with meditation, making it easier each time.

When you're meditating, make sure you're fully relaxed and focusing on the present moment. By focusing on your breathing, you are distracting yourself from any negative thoughts or feelings that may be overwhelming.

You can also use this time to visualize yourself living your dream life. The more vivid you can make it the better, because it will help to manifest your dream life.

However, it's important to remember that your

meditation practice is for you, and you can customize what you're doing depending on what kind of outcome you want. For example, you may want to meditate to;

- Release stress

- Practice visualization

- Clear your mind

- Better connect with the present moment

- Make peace with anxiety

- Explore potential solutions to problems

- Realize your goals

- Figure out what you want in life

- and much more

All these reasons to meditate will help you deepen your ability to use the Law of Attraction. So, for example, if you want to use meditation to visualize your future self and to have clarity with what you're trying to manifest, simply go through the steps above, making sure you're in a grounded and calm state of mind, tapping into your ability to focus.

In my own experience, I would get into this state of

mind after a few minutes, but it would still be challenging to stop thinking, so I chose to zero in on what those thoughts were. If it was really intense and my thoughts were traveling quickly, I would open my eyes and just write whatever came to mind, basically venting it all down onto the page.

If you want to visualize, follow the process, get into a calmer, more focused state of mind for a few minutes, perhaps ten minutes, and then practice visualizing. Use this state of mind to really feel whatever you want and what you're aiming for.

If you want answers to a problem, use meditation to explore certain avenues. See what comes up and when you find a potential answer, visualize it.

Whatever approach you take, whatever it is you want to do, and whatever you're trying to use the Law of Attraction for, make sure you're doing it every single day. Make meditation a routine. The more you practice, the better at it you'll become, and the better your connection will be with the law of attraction.

This is when you'll see the real results coming into your life.

Conclusion

And with that, you now know everything you need to know when it comes to using the Law of Attraction in all areas of your life. You know the logic and science behind the practice and the practical techniques you can use in your life.

I've managed to improve many areas of my life that I was least happy with simply by using techniques like meditation and visualization. If you do them regularly, you'll be amazed at how much more control you have over your own life, which is an incredible feeling!

However, it takes practice, and it takes consistency. This isn't just a process of writing down and focusing on what you want just one time. It's a life-changing process that doesn't really end.

It's the continual process of harnessing the power of your mind through repeated use that will open up new doors into areas that you never thought were possible. The best thing you can do is start the process and see the proof for yourself. It's all the motivation you'll need to continue.

That's all from me for now. As a final point of call, if you enjoyed reading this book, feel free to share your feedback, experiences, thoughts, or journey with this book by leaving a review at the store page where you picked up your copy and drop a comment in the review section.

I'll be reading everything posted, and I really look forward to hearing what you've got to say. I'm on my own journey of manifesting my passion, building my career, and becoming the best writer I can be, so I appreciate the time you've taken to not only read this book but also to get in touch.

And with that, I wish you all the best on your journey. These words will always be here if you need them, so feel free to come back any time.

Until next time!

Thank You

Before you go, I just wanted to say thank you for purchasing my book.

There are many books on the same topic, but you took a chance and chose this one.

So, thank you for choosing me and for reading this book all the way to the end.

Now, I wanted to ask you for a small favor. **Could you please consider posting a review for the book? Reviews are the easiest way to support an independent author like me.**

Your feedback will help me continue to create books that will help you achieve the results you want. So, if you enjoyed it, please let me know.

Thank You